IN c l e v e l a n d

Table of Contents

Staff

Rocco A. Di Lillo
President

Donna M. Shelley
Publisher

Laura A. Alosi
Arthur P. Fisher
Advertising

Ann M. Zoller
Editor

Van McCulloch
Diana Safos Thusat
Contributing Editors

Nesnadny & Schwartz
Design

Kathleen G. Lang
Office Manager

Kathleen Intihar
Executive Secretary

Typemasters, Inc.
Typesetting

Cleveland Advertising Club
Convention and Visitors Bureau
of Greater Cleveland
Greater Cleveland Growth
Association
Western Reserve Tourist Council
Memberships

Additional copies of **In Cleveland**
may be ordered by sending $18.95
per copy to the address below, or by
calling 1-800-234-2454, 9-5 EST,
Monday through Friday. VISA, MC,
AMEX; quantity discounts available.

In Cleveland is published annually
by City Visitor publications, P.O. Box
612, Hudson, Ohio 44236.
Copyright 1992. No part of this
publication may be reproduced or
duplicated without the express written
permission of the publisher.

In Cleveland, A Guide to the
City's Finest is designed to show-
case what the publishers feel are
some of the city's finest offerings.
Those represented in the book have
been chosen based on input from a
variety of sources, including our advi-
sory board. Some businesses have
been selected to receive extended
coverage and have paid an advertising fee for that exposure.

Money Creates Its Own Complications •

W E   S O R T   T H E M   O U T

Private Bankers for people with more complicated needs.

The courtesies go without saying. Significant credit and deposit

transactions are accommodated with our highest level of

personal attention and flexibility. Your needs merit our means.

Call Sandra Kiely, 575-2832.

One bank is not like all the rest.

NATIONAL CITY BANK

A National City Company

Cleve
landers

are as varied as our origins.

Yet there exist some common intangibles. We are **proud.**

We **work** hard. We **play** hard.

We **live** hard. We **try** harder.

We **appreciate.** We give.

We **dream** of

a pennant race. We say **hi** to strangers.

We have

heart.

We laugh a lot. We have treelawns.

We dream of the Super Bowl. We will **charm** you.

We want everyone to **like** Cleveland.

be
cause

we like Cleveland.

MICHAEL HEATON

"There's a real lack of phoniness in Cleveland, something out-of-towners pick up on right away."

Michael Heaton is The Minister of Culture. Albeit a self-proclaimed title and ministry, he is revered as such, and with good reason. Clevelanders need look no further than the preachings of the Minister found in The Plain Dealer's Friday and Sunday Magazines when searching for clues into the town's truly hip happenings. The following weekend, or an adaption thereof, is recommended for those looking to improve their cool quotient.

Highlights include: a run through Edgewater Park **. . . sushi at the east side's** Shujiro **restaurant . . . private parties at undisclosed locations with artistic types . . .** Major Hoopples River Bed Cafe **for some down-home, red-hot blues . . . a nightcap at the** Fulton Avenue Cafe **in Ohio City . . .** Steve's Lunch **on Lorain Avenue for some after-hours Slaw Dogs . . . a run through the wooded trails of Cleveland's expansive** Metroparks **. . . dinner in** Ohio City's Upstairs at the Fulton Avenue Cafe.

shopping

SOPHIS'

The architecturally spectacular Galleria at Erieview and The Avenue at Tower City Center are downtown's stellar shopping attractions. Both have elegant, chic stores and first rate service for the sophisticated patron.

For mall aficionados, the suburban selection and caliber is top-notch. From Beachwood's famous Beachwood Place mall to Rocky River's intimate Beachcliff Market Square there are numerous shopping facilities to suit individual tastes and temperaments.

If urban shopping is preferred, then take a stroll down Euclid Avenue from Public Square to E. 12th Street. The May Company and Higbee's, two of Cleveland's oldest and finest department stores, can be found there along with contemporary boutiques and specialty shops. The Arcade, a must-see treasured landmark, (stretching between Euclid and Superior avenues at E.6th Street) houses eateries and exclusive shops.

In addition to the malls and the downtown commercial district, Cleveland has several unique shopping locales. A trip to Chagrin Falls, a quaint eastern suburb, is a delightful excursion; the gazebo on the town square and natural waterfall add to its splendor. Coventry Road in Cleveland Heights, between Mayfield Road and Euclid Heights Boulevard, is another worthwhile trek. Ethnically and economically diverse, it's a stone's-throw away from University Circle. And Shaker Square, on Cleveland's east side is an eclectic mix of fascinating shops.

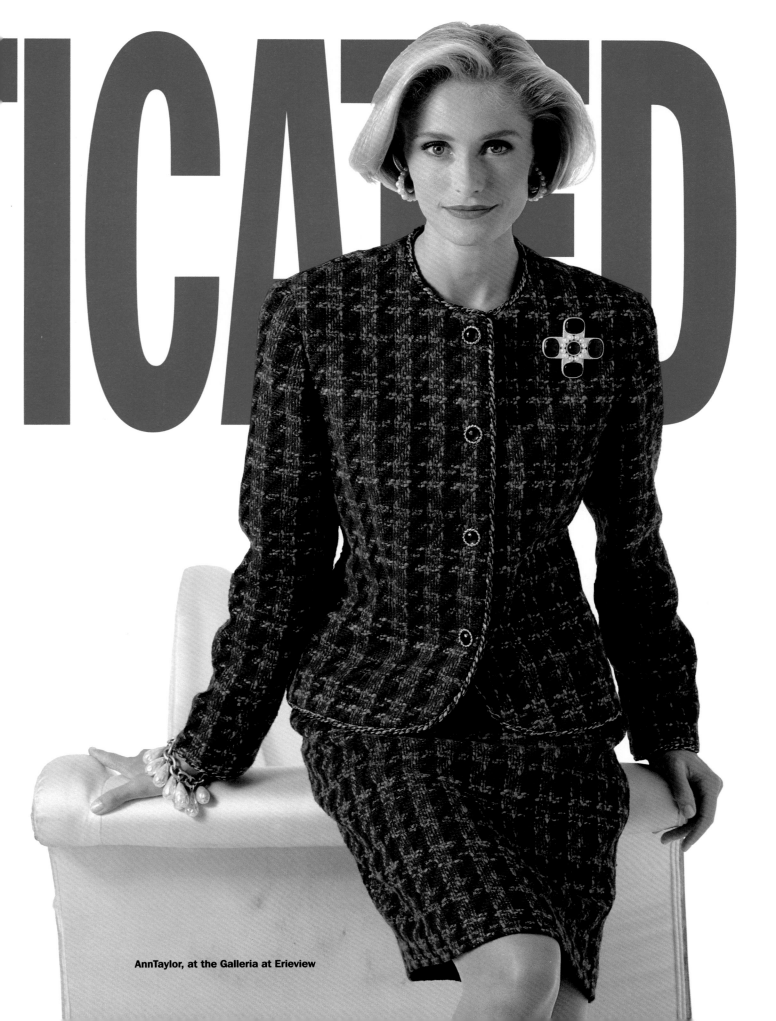

ICATED

AnnTaylor, at the Galleria at Erieview

POTTER AND MELLEN, INC.

One-of-a-kind 14 K. gold intaglio necklace with pearls and matching earrings, designed and crafted by Potter and Mellen.

Potter and Mellen, Inc.
10405 Carnegie Avenue
in University Circle,
next to the Omni Hotel/Cleveland Clinic
231-5100

Mon-Sat 9:30-5

Potter and Mellen, Inc. has been Cleveland's carriage trade jeweler and silversmith of choice since 1899. Master craftsmen design and create internationally-acclaimed jewelry and silver holloware on the premises. Many of these pieces are in permanent collections of major art museums throughout the world. Fine and exquisite gem and gold jewelry are the basis of Potter and Mellen's reputation for excellence, and its extensive collection of silver jewelry is well known throughout the city.

The visitor to Potter and Mellen will find distinctive and exclusive gift lines such as Buccellati, Baccarat, and Tiffany in its merchandise, which includes stationery, clocks, dinnerware, silver flatware and holloware, crystal stemware and holloware, linens and baby gifts.

Quality services include the redesign or repair of heirloom jewelry, engraving, the design of medals or presentation gifts, appraisals and signature gift wrap.

The Ellen Stirn Galleries, Inc. - located in Potter and Mellen - features 18th & 19th Century European decorative arts, including porcelain, silver, crystal and prints. All pieces are personally selected by Ellen in Europe, with each piece being researched and displayed as a work of art. Major exhibitions are held four times throughout the year.

"Potter and Mellen is committed to continuing historic and classic designs as well as selecting or designing tomorrow's classics."

Ellen Stirn Mavec, President

James Clothiers offers the finest in contemporary men's fashions. Located conveniently at The Pavilion in Beachwood, James Clothiers is an elegant shopping experience. Rich woods, soft lighting and stunning architecture create an inviting milieu for choosing from an impressive selection of today's top fashions for men. Updated traditional looks, continental clothing and popular Euro-fashions define the look and feel of James Clothiers. James Clothiers is a must for any man looking for quality, comfortable clothing which reflects not only the trends of the time, but his own personal style.

James Clothiers
The Pavilion
24119 Chagrin Blvd.
Beachwood
831-6470

Mon-Sat 10-6
Tues & Thur 10-9
Sun 12-5

"James Clothiers offers contemporary fashions for men who pride themselves on their own good taste-in a setting designed for those who appreciate comfort."

Jim Bradlin, owner

"Everyone wants to think they have something no one else has...and it will last forever. I give them that. I know it." IMG

Photography by Benjamin Margalit

JEWELS BY IMG

Jewels By IMG, Inc.
5470 Mayfield Rd.
Lyndhurst
461-9550
1-800-321-6317

Owner IMG is nationally known for his unique, award-winning designs and gracious demeanor. His premier jewelry salon is intensively customer oriented, offering personal consultations in private sitting rooms.

Showroom hours Mon- Fri 9:30 am to 5:30 pm, Sat 9 am-5pm
Tueday evening only by appointment
Special designs by appointment.

**Transportation provided
to and from hotels**

International dignitaries and celebrities such as Liberace and Sammy Davis, Jr. and sports stars such as Nate Thurmond and Austin Carr have come to IMG for exclusive jewelry. All pieces are custom made on the premises by craftsmen using the finest precious stones and metals. Work is done in 14k and 18k gold and platinum. Specialty items include rings for the arthritic and gold braille watches.

This award winning re-adaptation and expansion of a 1930s movie theatre is in the genre of Ghirardelli Square in San Francisco and Faneuil Hall Marketplace in Boston. It is Cleveland's specialty shopping source for fine clothing and jewelry, personal services ranging from hair styling to skin care, and incomparable giftware and home furnishings. As you consider your purchases, sample the Euro-American cuisine of Heck's Cafe or the Szechuan sauces of Pearl of the Orient, two of Cleveland's consistently top rated restaurants. Explore the offerings of 26 shops with the personal assistance of shopkeepers who have searched the market places of the world for uncommon excellence. Beachcliff Market Square is still a showplace.

BEACHCLIFF
MARKET SQUARE

Beachcliff Market Square
19300 Detroit Road
Rocky River
333-5074

Explore the offerings of 26 shops with the personal assistance of shopkeepers who have searched the market places of the world for uncommon excellence.

Open Tues.-Fri. 10 am-9 pm; Mon. & Sat. 10 am to 5:30 pm; Sundays during the holiday season 12 pm to 5 pm.

"My customers share an appreciation for fine clothing and customized service in an unhurrried, uncommon atmosphere for gentlemen's and ladies apparel."

Wally Naymon, owner.

Kilgore Trout
On the east side at the
Eton Collection
28601 Chagrin Blvd.
831-0488

Open Mon.- Sat 10 am to 6 pm;
Thursday 10 am to 9 pm
AE, MC and Visa accepted

Transportation provided
to and from hotels

For 14 years, Cleve-landers have known that Kilgore Trout is the place for clothing with a smashing sense of taste and style. Each customer receives the personal service to find just the piece or ensemble for which they are looking. Suits, separates, sportswear, tailored clothing and accessories are available for both men and women, while formal-wear and shoes are available for men only.

A wide range of top designer lines such as Ermenegildo Zegna, Giorgio Armani, Verri, Byblos, Dino Valiano, and Iceberg are carried by Kilgore Trout, in addition to its own exclusive Italian-made line, Moda Firenze. Custom tailoring for men and free alter-ations for both men and women are also available.

Outfit by Dino Valiano

KILGORE TROUT

While in Cleveland, drop in on some famous names.

The Limited

Cleveland Indians Gift Shop

AnnTaylor

Eddie Bauer

Williams–Sonoma

Talbots

No matter what brings you to Cleveland — be it business or pleasure or a little of both — there's one place that's a "must shop." The Galleria at Erieview with 60 great fashion and specialty shops. 12 places to eat including Ninth Street Grill and Sweetwater's Café Sausalito. And, the "official and only" Cleveland Indians Gift Shop. So, while in Cleveland, drop in on some great shopping. Galleria at Erieview.

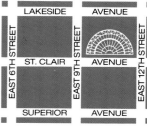

GALLERIA
AT ERIEVIEW

Drop by our customer service center for your free Cleveland souvenir and Galleria at Erieview gift bag.

Open Daily 10 am to 8 pm
Saturdays 10 am to 7 pm
Sundays and Holidays 11 am to 6 pm
Restaurants open extended hours

The Galleria's numerous stores make it a wonderful destination for serious shopping, while the spacious design is perfect for a lazy afternoon of leisurely browsing.

For convenience, accessibility, and a pleasant environment, nothing beats a leisurely shopping excursion to the Galleria at Erieview. A ten minute walk from both Public Square and the downtown lakeshore, this four-year-old structure is known for its spectacular design. Natural light is filtered through a glass arched roof onto marble floors and sixty-foot columns. Discriminating patrons can find designer fashions, leather wear, sports shoes, travel and safari clothing, jewelry, fine fragrances, records, books, luggage, candy, gourmet cookware and a host of other distinctive goods.

A sunlit food court offers a variety of fast food eateries, and restaurants Sweetwater's Cafe Sausalito and Ninth Street Grill offer extensive menus for fine dining. An underground parking garage is accessible off Lakeside Avenue, and Valet Parking is available at both the E. 9th Street and E. 12th Street entrances. In addition, shuttle service provides transportation from the restaurants to Playhouse Square for theater performances.

Eddie Bauer

Cleveland Indians Gift Shop

Galleria at Erieview
Downtown,
E. 9th Street at
St. Clair Avenue
621-9999

23

FENA'S

Fena's Skin Care Clinic, Inc.
21625 Chagrin Blvd.
Suite 200
Beachwood
561-FENA (3362)

For the woman who truly enjoys the gentle art of pampering, there is but one solution—Fena's. Fena's Skin Care Clinic offers an atmosphere of quiet relaxation, with full-service beauty care for women only. For hair styles, facials, massage, and manicures, Fena's offers total body care by European trained aestheticians. The products used contain only natural ingredients

Open Mon. - Sat. 9 a.m. to 6 p.m.;
Thursdays 9 a.m. to 9 p.m.
By appointment only.

and all treatments are administered on an individual basis in private rooms. A wide variety of deep cleansing facial, body and skin treatments, body waxing, hair care, and smile enhancement services (provided by Dr. H.N. Silverman) are available. Changing rooms, a lunch room, Jacuzzi and shower are located on the premises for each customer's complete comfort.

"Every woman deserves to lose herself for a day, to indulge in pampering and experience the relaxing, revitalizing effects of total beauty care."

Fena, president

WILMA SMITH

"**Being a life-long Clevelander, I never miss an opportunity to tout the city.**"

"Home grown" Wilma Smith is a welcome guest in thousands of homes in Cleveland. Her familiar smiling visage brightens Cleveland's outlook no matter what the news. Viewers of News Channel 5 are drawn to Wilma's natural appeal with good reason - it's pure Cleveland. Born and raised on the North Coast, Wilma has countless ideas for showing off her hometown.

Highlights of Wilma's busy weekend include: cocktails and appetizers at Gamekeepers Taverne in Chagrin Falls . . . dinner and dancing at nearby Hunters Hollow . . . lunch at Theresa's Italian Cuisine in Little Italy . . . University Circle's museums – including The Garden Center, The Cleveland Museum of Art and The Museum of Natural History . . . dinner at Chez Francois in Vermilion . . . Sunday brunch at Thistledown Racing Club . . . the Cleveland Metroparks Zoo . . . a sunset cruise aboard the beautiful Goodtime III . . . a day to relax and indulge at Mario's Aurora House Spa with dinner at The Waterford Room.

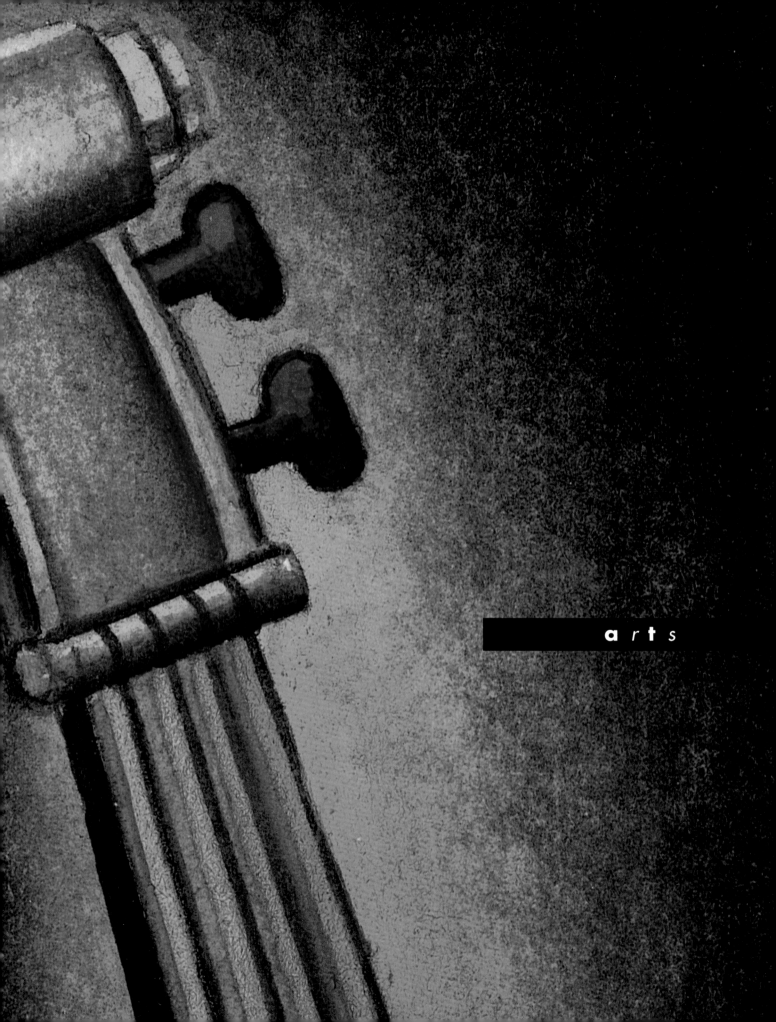

arts

Cleveland's artistic

community flourishes in

one of the country's most

conducive environments

for creative expression.

By Diana Safos Thusat

Bull's Skull, Fruit, Pitcher. Pablo Picasso, oil on canvas, 1939. The Cleveland Museum of Art, Leonard C. Hanna, Jr., Fund 85.57

esthetes of the world will be happy to find Greater Cleveland's cultural life in a healthy, vigorous condition. Both the performing and visual arts are well represented and are thriving under public and corporate support and appreciation.

What a glorious town this is for dazzling entertainment ranging from Broadway productions to Cleveland's own world renowned orchestra. Be it is classical, contemporary or avant-garde, Cleveland offers the best in music, theater and dance.

One of the city's greatest treasures is **The Cleveland Orchestra.** Established in 1918, it is respected internationally as being one of the world's finest. Its reputation for excellence grew under the direction of George Szell, who was the conductor from 1946 to 1970. Szell embarked on several extensive foreign tours with the orchestra, as well as expanding its commercial recording repertoire.

Currently, The Cleveland Orchestra is under the direction of conductor Christoph von Dohnányi, whose praises have been sung by many music critics, such as Andrew Porter of The New Yorker, "Wisdom, judgement, strength of personality, and integrity of feeling mark his work. Uncommon technical accomplishment also plays its part: under Dohnányi's leadership, the Cleveland is again what it was under Szell—one of the world's great orchestras."

The Cleveland Orchestra performs at **Severance Hall** in University Circle from September through May. During the summer months, the orchestra plays in the open-air amphitheater at Blossom Music Center, and makes special appearances at venues such as North Coast Harbor and Nautica Stage.

Head west of University Circle toward downtown Cleveland to find the **Playhouse Square Center.** This group of three renovated theaters, the Ohio, Palace, and State, is the third largest entertainment complex in North America, and consistently draws first-rate performers.

The Cleveland Orchestra at Nautica Stage

The Crawford Auto-Aviation Museum

Playhouse Square Foundation, the organization that manages the theaters, has become a nationally recognized incubator of new American musical productions as well as a successful producer.

To date the company has produced and presented the acclaimed *Gospel at Colonus* on Broadway after initiating the production at the State Theater, and co-produced *Big River* and *Pump Boys & Dinettes* for national tour.

The Playhouse Square Foundation has presented hundreds of pop entertainers, comedians, touring musicals and international attractions including: the Rat Pack with Frank Sinatra and Sammy Davis, Jr., the Legends of Comedy with Milton Berle, Danny Thomas and Sid Ceasar; the Manhattan Transfer; *Phantom of the Opera; Cats;* and *Les Miserables.*

The theaters themselves are worth visiting just to enjoy their magnificent architecture and loving restorations. The three theaters were built in the 1920s as vaudeville houses and are listed on the National Register of Historic Places. The

renovation of the theaters, at a cost of $37.7 million, has distinguished Playhouse Square Center as the largest theater restoration project in the world.

Playhouse Square also hosts several resident companies including the Cleveland Ballet, Great Lakes Theater Festival and Cleveland Opera.

Founded by Dennis Nahat and Ian Horvath, former American Ballet dancers, the **Cleveland Ballet** is the fifth largest ballet company in the nation. Known in California as San Jose Cleveland Ballet, the company is recognized for performances in the grand theatrical style. Its ever-widening choreography by Bournonville, Flindt, Limon, Lichine, Balanchine, and deMille. The Cleveland Ballet performs matinees and evenings at the State Theater.

The **Great Lakes Theater Festival,** founded by Arthur Lithgow, will celebrate it 30th anniversary in July 1992. The Festival presents classics of all theatrical eras—from the poetry of Shakespeare to the wit of Shaw, from the emotion of Chekov and Ibsen to the melodies of Broadway's golden age. Utilizing the beautifully appointed Ohio Theater as its home, it continues to attract the country's finest talents. (Tom Hanks performed with the company in the late 1970s.)

The **Cleveland Opera** celebrates it 15th anniversary this year. Formed as the city's resident opera company, it first sought to develop a strong audience base by performing most of its works in English. Also appealing to the masses is its repertoire, which will please both neophytes and opera aficionados. Classics such as Faust and Aida have been performed as well as the operettas *Naughty Marietta* and *Kiss Me, Kate.*

Another long-standing member of Cleveland's performing arts community is **The Cleveland Play House.** Founded in 1915, it is the country's oldest regional (professional, non-profit) theater. The Play House's three theaters, the Bolton, Brooks and Drury, are housed in one complex which was designed by internationally acclaimed architect Philip Johnson. It stretches between Euclid and Carnegie avenues at East 86th Street.

The Cleveland Play House is committed to artistic achievement and has nurtured prominent actors such as Joel Grey, Ray Walston, Alan Alda, Margaret Hamilton and Dom DeLuise. Today, the theater continues to stage first-rate production with talented entertainers such as Marlo Thomas, Daniel J. Travanti, Bill Cobbs, Tammy Grimes and Joe Mascolo. Currently under the artistic direction of Josephine R. Abady, the Play House continues to attract national recognition for its commitment to producing new American plays.

Walk down the street to East 89th and Quincy Avenue to find another Cleveland treasure, **Karamu House.** Founded in 1915 by white social workers Rowena and Russell Jelliffe, the theater was committed to interracial artistic productions at a time when segregation was the norm. Karamu, which is Swahili for "a place of joyful meeting," continues to serve the black community by promoting new artistic endeavors.

State Theatre

Palace Theatre

At Playhouse Square Center, the theaters themselves are worth visiting just to enjoy their magnificent architecture and loving restoration.

Museums

Cleveland's rich cultural heritage is nowhere more visible than through its collection of acclaimed museums. No other city in the world offers such a dense concentration of cultural institutions as Cleveland's **University Circle** area. A proud legacy of monetary and land bequests from area philanthropists stands behind the five major museums.

The Cleveland Museum of Art, began a year-long celebration of its 75th anniversary in 1991. The Museum, which opened its doors to the public on June 6, 1916, is one of the finest in the country and its prestigious collections are world famous. More than 48,000 works of art representing a wide range of cultures and periods are permanently on display.

Noted for its impressive collection of Asian and Medieval European artwork, The Cleveland Museum of Art also boasts an outstanding array of Egyptian, Greek, Roman, African, and pre-Columbian art. The Cleveland Museum of Art is a private and non-profit institution.

Another institution devoted to the public is **The Cleveland Museum of Natural History.** Founded in 1920 by local attorney Harold Clark, the Museum's purpose was, and is, to enable people to understand and appreciate our physical environment. It is the largest museum in Ohio dedicated specifically to natural history, conservation and environmental education.

Located on the edge of Wade Oval across the street from the Art Museum, the Cleveland Museum of Natural History contains four large display galleries, a living-animal section, a planetarium, an observatory, a research library, an auditorium and temporary exhibit galleries.

The Museum's most popular exhibitions are reconstructed prehistoric animals, which especially thrill and delight children.

The Cleveland Play House

Dinosaurs, a giant elk, a saber-toothed cat and an American mastodon stand as reminders of the Ice Age. Special exhibits highlighting an array of prehistoric creatures always attract record crowds.

Another museum complex on the edge of Wade Oval is **The Western Reserve Historical Society,** which is comprised of the History Museum, History Library, and Crawford Auto-Aviation Museum. Founded in 1867, the Historical Society is the oldest existing cultural institution in Cleveland. Open year-round, it is the largest privately supported regional historical collection in the country. Among its original benefactors were John D. Rockefeller, Charles Baldwin and Charles Whittlesey.

The History Museum is housed in two magnificent early-20th century mansions. Both homes are Italian Renaissance in style and feature exquisite architectural detailing, woodwork, ironwork and large formal gardens. Extensive collections of American furniture and decorative arts are displayed in more than 20 period rooms which highlight the finest in American and European furnishings from the mid-18th century to the 1920s. Glass, silver, ceramics, costumes, paintings and domestic implements are located throughout the Museum and in special exhibition galleries and displays.

The Crawford Auto-Aviation Museum contains more than 150 antique, vintage and classic automobiles, motorcycles and rare aircraft. It was opened in 1965 after receiving a collection of historical automobiles and aircraft from TRW, Inc.

Included in the museum's collection is the oldest closed automobile known to exist in North America, an 1895 Panhard et Levassor. A more recent addition is a 1981 Aston Martin Lagonda. These cars and the entire collection represent the technological and stylistic advancement of the automobile.

The Cleveland Museum of Natural History

The Garden Center of Greater Cleveland

While not properly a museum, **The Garden Center of Greater Cleveland,** which also sits on the edge of Wade Oval, is another worthwhile stop. It is the oldest civic garden center in the United States and contains the largest garden center library in the country. Founded in 1930, The Garden Center was "to offer a place where all people may come for information on landscape problems, where people may study books and data on gardens, flowers, plant life, and landscape work, where monthly exhibits may illustrate and instruct in the art of gardening."

In fulfilling its mission to educate the public about flora, The Garden Center conducts tours, lectures, classes, workshops, and clinics for gardeners, home owners, and specialists.

A visitor who ventures a few blocks west of University Circle can find the **Cleveland Health Education Museum** on Euclid Avenue. Founded in 1936 to help educate the public on health related matters, this is the oldest permanent health museum in the country.

The Museum promotes well-being in all areas of life. Its goal is to educate the individual as well as the health care professional. It generated the nation's first sex education class for elementary and secondary children, and was a pioneer in drug education. The Museum developed programs for the elderly and the disabled.

The Cleveland Health Education Museum galleries were designed for dramatic visual appeal, while retaining scholarly integrity. "See, hear, and touch" is the rule in this hands-on environment. The challenge for the museum is to translate an idea into an educational participatory display.

Another user-friendly museum in the area is the **Cleveland Children's Museum.** Located in University Circle on Euclid Avenue, this Museum was opened in 1986 for children between the ages 3-12. The Museum is a multi-sensory, creative learning environment with three room-sized exhibits which parents and kids can enjoy through hands-on experience and a range of learning opportunities. Exhibits incorporate more than 100 activities through manipulating objects, role playing and fantasy, and social interaction.

Smaller but equally intriguing area museums outside of University Circle include the African-American Museum, Cleveland Police Historical Society Museum, Great Lakes Historical Society, and Harriet Tubman Museum & Cultural Association.

Galleries

Cleveland Institute of Art

Holy Family on the Steps. Nicolas Poussin, oil on canvas, 1648.
The Cleveland Museum of Art, Leonard C. Hanna, Jr., Fund 81.18

The opportunity for artists to create and display their works in Cleveland has never been better. With both traditional spaces and a variety of non-traditional exhibition areas, all forms and styles of art can find a niche in the city.

One especially strong artistic enclave is Cleveland's University Circle and it adjacent neighborhood, Little Italy. Artists are able to live, work and exhibit their creations in this culturally distinct district. The fountainheads for much of this area's art is the **Cleveland Institute of Art.** The Institute takes pride in its students' works, which are presented for public viewing during the school's periodic showings. The Reinberger Galleries, with 5,000 sq. ft., is the second largest gallery in Cleveland. Another institutional gallery in the area is Case Western Reserve University's **Mather Gallery.** Eight shows are organized each year from September through May. The gallery's special curatorial interests include contemporary sculpture, Black Art, and performing art. Items can be purchased directly through the gallery; three weeks after a show closes buyers are directed to the individual artists.

Up the hill in the quaint Little Italy neighborhood, several distinct art galleries line Murray Hill Road. **Avante Gallery,** which is operated by ceramic artist Tom Huck, displays only three-dimensional art. With a healthy balance between regional and national artists, the gallery offers contemporary, expressionistic ceramic, glass and sculpted pieces. The gallery promotes progressive work and art that is created by using obscure media.

Fiori Studio Gallery, operated by handmade paper artists David Batz and Robert Jursinski, carries a broad range of contemporary regional and national artwork. From paintings and crafts to photographs, this combined shop and gallery values all forms of artistic expression. In addition to its six shows per year, the gallery participates in the Murray Hill Art Walks, held the first weeks of December and June of each year.

Riley Hawk Galleries represents prominent national and international glass artists such as Dale Chihuly, Harvey Littleton, William Morris, Steve Weinberg and William Carlson. Jewelry, sculptures, vases and paper weights are displayed during the gallery's six annual shows. One-person shows scheduled for this year include the following artists: Jose Chardiet, Paul Stankard, Steve Weinberg, and Bill Carlson.

William Busta Gallery, also located on Murray Hill Road, is a bit unusual for Cleveland in that it focuses on a small stable of local artists. Busta's commitment to the development of the artists is comparable to galleries in larger art markets such as New York, Los Angeles and Chicago. Painters, print makers, sculptors, photographers and tapestry artists are represented individually in the gallery's eleven yearly shows. Cleveland's downtown also contains numerous art galleries including **The Bonfoey Company,** which has served Cleveland for 98 years. The gallery specializes in 19th and 20th century paintings and prints, contemporary artwork, art restoration, carving and gilding, distinctive framing, fine art shipping, art consultations and appraisals.

<u>Coffin Case and Cover of Bekenmut.</u> Egypt, Thebes, ca. 1070-945 BC. Wood with gesso and paint. The Cleveland Museum of Art, Gift of the John Huntington Art and Polytechnic Trust 14.561

In the historic Warehouse District the **Brenda Kroos Gallery** displays the works of contemporary, nationally known artists. Paintings, fine art, limited editions and reproductions are included in its six annual shows. The gallery also handles corporate sales and individual consultations. Owner Brenda Kroos, intending to educate the public on contemporary art, encourages people to browse as they would in a museum.

While not precisely a gallery, also in the Warehouse District is **Wolf's Fine Art Auctioneers,** one of only ten fine arts auctioneers in the United States. The auction house holds 12 specialty auctions per year including an Important Art Glass and Decorative Arts Auction, a Prints and Drawing Auction, and an American and European Painting and Sculpture Auction.

The Cleveland Center For Contemporary Art

Another noteworthy downtown gallery is **SPACES.** Founded in 1977, SPACES serves as a forum for avant-garde art in Northeast Ohio. The gallery created opportunities for emerging local and regional artists to present their work to the public. SPACES exhibits any art that is new, unconventional and non-traditional, including video, film, dance, music, poetry, performance art and anything else that seems challenging.

In addition to those clustered in University Circle, Little Italy and downtown, Cleveland has many other notable galleries dispersed throughout the area. **Sylvia Ullman American Crafts Gallery** focuses on the national art scene and exhibits primarily contemporary works. Established 27 years ago, it is one of the country's largest galleries and enjoys an outstanding reputation. Special shows include Art in the Garden, the National Furniture Invitational, and the National Ceramic Invitational.

Vixseboxse Art Galleries in Cleveland Heights is one of the area's oldest galleries dealing exclusively in 19th century and early 20th century fine art. This third generation run gallery owns most of its inventory of American and European paintings, watercolors and prints.

Eleven-year-old **Malcolm Brown Gallery,** in neighboring Shaker Heights, is a full service gallery renowned for quality art and service. It showcases artists of regional and national prominence including Romare Bearden, Elizabeth Catlett and Hughie Lee-Smith. Museum quality paintings, graphics, sculptures, and African contemporary pieces are on display during the gallery's eight annual shows.

The **Cleveland Center for Contemporary Art,** located in the Cleveland Play House, is celebrating its 24th year of presenting nationally known contemporary artists. The Center considers public education and awareness of art an important part of its mission.

Riley Hawk Galleries

2026 Murray Hill Road
Little Italy/University Circle
421-1445

One of the top art galleries in America, featuring museum quality art expressed in glass, Riley Hawk is riding the crest of a new wave in glass art.

Because the United States leads the world in the refinement and creation of glass art, that places the gallery in the vanguard internationally. In turn, glass art itself leads the worldwide three-dimensional art movement.

This explosion in three-dimensional glass art began 30 years ago in Toledo, Ohio with Harvey Littleton, who is considered the father of the modern glass art surge. Littleton's work, as well as that of his proteges and other internationally revered glass artists, can be seen at Riley Hawk. The emphasis of the gallery is on quality, contemporary art by artists whose pieces have been purchased by the Louvre, the Metropolitan Museum of Art and other internationally acclaimed museums.

What makes glass art especially exciting today is the maturity of the field; according to Riley, "The materials are much more sophisticated today then they were 30 years ago."

Riley Hawk emphasizes in-depth works of internationally renowned glass artists such as Harvey Littleton, Dale Chihuly, Christopher Ries, Jon Kuhn, Paul Stankard, Damian Priour, William Morris, Steve Weinberg, William Carlson, Dan Dailey, Paul Manners, José Chardiet, Ben Tré, Rothenfeld, and Lipofsky. Most artists displayed at Riley Hawk Galleries hold Masters Degrees from America's leading universities.

Riley's personal commitment to the artists and the gallery comes from a deep appreciation of glass art and a commitment to the aesthetic quality of life in Greater Cleveland. His special pride in the city and its cultural milieu is reflected in Riley Hawk Galleries.

If you would like to receive information on upcoming shows, please call the gallery and request to be added to the mailing list.

The emphasis of the gallery is on quality, contemporary art by artists whose pieces have been purchased by the Louvre, the Metropolitan Museum of Art and other internationally acclaimed museums.

Riley Hawk is considered to be one of America's foremost authorities in glass art.

Spring Blossom, by Jon Kuhn

"Nothing is more romantic than enjoying a quiet weekend close to home, enjoying all of our favorite sights, sounds, tastes and attractions."

When looking to plan a romantic weekend, we looked no further than the footlights at Playhouse Square to find **Karen Gabay and Raymond Rodriguez**, principal dancers for the Cleveland Ballet. This dreamy duo has captivated audiences not only with their inspired dance but with their real life love story—as husband and wife. As performing artists who travel frequently, comfort and relaxation are at the focus of this cozy weekend made for two.

Highlights of this weekend for two include: a Broadway production at Playhouse Square . . . a leisurely continental breakfast at Truffles and a walk along Edgewater Park, on Cleveland's west side . . . a Mexican fare fiesta at Lopez y Gonzalez . . . big band dancing at Aquilon in the Flats . . . Mass at St. John's Cathedral downtown . . . brunch at Pier W on the lake . . . a drive through Cleveland's gracious suburbs . . . dinner at Shujiro, The Restaurant of Japan.

"Cleveland has such a vital, healthy cultural community, with something for every passion."

As Artistic Director for The Cleveland Play House, Josephine Abady has a hands-on knowledge of what's happening in the town's cultural and artistic scene. Under Josie's careful direction, any weekend in Cleveland is sure to garner a standing ovation. The following spotlights her own unique playbill for fun and adventure.

Josie's weekend would include: dinner at the Baricelli Inn and a performance by The Cleveland Orchestra at Severance Hall . . . brunch at The Ritz-Carlton . . . a tour of Tower City and the Galleria at Erieview . . . lunch at Sammy's in the Flats . . . a Lolly the Trolley tour of downtown . . . dinner at The Play House Club followed by a Cleveland Play House production . . . brunch at James Tavern . . . a tour of The Cleveland Museum of Art and the Center for Contemporary Art . . . dinner at Pier W.

KAREN RAYMOND

JOSIE ABADY

cuisine

Todd and Donn Carmel, Proprietors

Getty's

Two Restaurants, One Famous Name

Legendary among locals and increasingly among sophisticated visitors, the two Getty's restaurants help define the meaning of truly fine dining in Cleveland. The Carmel brothers, Todd and Donn, blend three decades of experience into a single and unwavering commitment to quality both at Getty's at the Hanna and Getty's in Westlake. **Getty's at the Hanna,** in the heart of Cleveland's Playhouse Square, presents an appropriately dramatic decor.

Fluted columns support a high ceiling decorated with Hellenic-Romanesque characters, and etched glass partitions create the intimacy of dining alcoves. **At** intermission time in the three theatres across the street, playgoers patronize the Chicago-style bar at Getty's. Dinner-theatre packages are available as is an after-theatre menu. **Todd** Carmel is the proprietor of this popular downtown rendezvous where dining room patrons are entertained by live piano Wednesday through Sunday evenings. **Late** night entertainment at Playhouse Square is further enhanced by a visit to Rhythms,

downtown's newest hot-spot. Adjacent to Getty's, this premier jazz club offers live music Thursday through Saturday evenings. National acts are featured at Rhythms on a special event basis. **Getty's West,** where Donn Carmel presides, has a relaxing, hospitable ambiance that is immensely popular with fun-loving, contemporary adults. They find a special kind of camaraderie both on the unique summer patio and in the attractive lounge. **The** two establishments feature many of the same favorite dishes. Eclectic menus stress the chef's daily creations and several entree salads. Salad Brittany, for one, is a bed of bibb lettuce and radicchio crowned with grilled chicken, bacon, almonds and warm French brandy dressing. Dinner entrees include a number of beef dishes such as Blackened Strip Steak. Getty's is also famous for superb main dishes like Veal St. Jacques, Chicken Forestiere, Shrimp Romano and several fresh seafood selections. **Getty's** boasts a large wine cellar as well as an outstanding selection of ports and cognac.

1. **at the Hanna** 2. **West**

By Van McCulloch　　Photography by Beth Segal

"Come and find out why

it took a lifetime to create

The Burgess

Grand Cafe."

Paul Martoccia, Proprietor

The Burgess Grand Cafe, Downtown
1406 W. 6th **574-2232**

Serving breakfast & lunch.......................... Monday-Friday
Dinner 7 days a week...........................starting at 5:30 pm
Sunday Brunch ....from 11 to 3pm

At The Burgess Grand Cafe, "grand" is not just a word; it's a philosophy. Grand is the quintessence of fine dining. Elegant presentaion of food. Splendid surroundings. A reminder of an era when perfect service was taken for granted.

Just a short walk from Public Square in the historic Warehouse District, the restaurant is a popular rendezvous for Clevelanders. They are attracted by a wide-ranging menu including Northern Italian dishes with freshly made pasta, duck breast, sweetbreads, fresh seafood and filet of tenderloin. A cellar well- stocked with domestic and imported wines adds to the enjoyment.

Even the regulars never tire of the beautiful surroundings. They dine on tables topped with imported rose-colored marble; sip from black stemmed wine goblets; admire the provocative wall murals that were commissioned by the proprietor, Paul Martoccia.

Breakfast, usually an elusive meal, is not only available here, it's a work of art. Offerings like Oatmeal Pecan Pancakes and Orange Brandied French Toast give a special jumpstart to the power breakfast. A bountiful Sunday Brunch is also available.

Light menus are featured in the lounge where a jazz trio performs Wednesday, Friday and Saturday evenings.

Reservations are recommended for those who want to experience this eminently upscale establishment.

Classics

Classics - a name not casually bestowed. A name signifying tradition. Refinement. Excellence that withstands the test of time.

Classics, then, is the perfect name for a restaurant that is clearly one of the most elegant in the entire area. Located adjacent to the Omni Hotel, Classics is accustomed to hosting celebrities and royalty from around the world. It is also the only Cleveland restaurant that AAA has once again judged worthy of its coveted Four-Diamond rating.

A classic menu disregards transient trends in favor of fresh, satisfying food that is always in fashion. Special entrees include such favorites as Veal Oscar and Chateaubriand. The tableside menu includes Steak Diane and Rack of Lamb. The culinary brigade adds the creative touch with a host of sauces and fresh seafood daily. Spa selections are also available. The appetizers and desserts, presented like fine art, are extraordinary.

Diners are serenaded by piano and strings in a flower-filled setting that achieves an atmosphere of relaxation amid all the elegance. Enjoy complimentary valet parking. Advance reservations and proper attire required.

Classics, adjacent to the Omni Hotel, Carnegie at E. 96th St. 791-1300

Serving lunch **Monday through Friday 11:30-2:30**

Dinner **Monday through Thursday 5:30-10 Friday & Saturday 5:30-10:30**

Closed on Sunday

AmethystGrille

Although technically a semi-precious stone, the amethyst has a surprisingly unique appeal. Its namesake restaurant is also a gem. Crystal- studded walls at The Amethyst Grille are a jewel box full of sparkling surprises.

The stunning decor spotlights large specimens of amethyst mounted in niches along stark, white walls. The violet motif, mingled with grey and dusty rose, continues in the table settings. Music is gentle and - surprise!- it typically is live.

Entree selections range from grilled chops to poultry, prawns and pasta. In its performance with steaks and fish, however, lies the kitchen's true tour-de-force.

George Hwang and **Rose Wong,** Proprietors

"Since being voted best new restaurant in Esquire Magazine, we are determined to continue deserving such accolades. Our customers tell us we've been getting even better."

283-1800

**20123 Van Aken Blvd.
Shaker Heights**

**Serving lunch & dinner
Mon.-Sat. starting at 11:30 am
Open Sun. 5 to 10 pm**

Grilled Teppanyaki Filet Mignon, for one, is testimony to the kitchen's creativity as well as its respect for the star of steakdom. Drifted with sesame seeds and served over grilled marinated onions, the meat's superior qualities are not muted, just subtly enhanced.

Innovative touches are also evident in the seven choices of fresh fish offered daily. Among the most popular is Broiled Coho Salmon with Mushroom Spinach Stuffing and a Lime Cumin Glaze. Grilled Mahi Mahi, crowned with Honey- Tamari-Sesame Sauce, is also stellar.

Guests wishing to enhance their dining experience with wine will find suggestions listed with most entrees. While connoisseurs may at first be amazed by the depth of the Amethyst wine cellar, it's but another facet of this gourmet gem.

49

The Legions of Regulars who frequent the Watermark know they can count on one thing - that the restaurant is never the same place twice. Spectacular scenery, viewed from indoors or from the River Patio, is an ever-changing kaleidoscope of activity and watercraft. The menu is also changed every day to reflect the freshest bounties of the marketplace. **With** the same certainty, patrons also know that some things never change. The kitchen takes uncompromising pride in food preparation; no short cuts here. Everything from bread and salad dressings to devastating desserts is prepared "from scratch" on the premises. Also ever-present is the ambiance of laid-back, casual elegance.

The Outdoor Patio, one of Cleveland's finest, is famous not only for the view but for its romantic culinary experience. Gas heaters provide comfort even when the weather turns chilly. **As** befits a riverfront restaurant, impeccably fresh fish and seafood are kings of the menu. The kitchen gives preferential treatment to its royalty. Delicacies such as mahi mahi, grouper, trout, tuna, salmon, swordfish, amberjack or kajiki may be sauteed, baked or marinated, then gently grilled on smoky-sweet mesquite. Landlubbers can find friendly fare, too, on a menu that is stunning in its scope and variety. Prices are surprisingly moderate for food and service of such unwavering quality.

Watermark Restaurant
1250 Old River Road
in the Flats **241-1600**

The Wine List, one of Cleveland's most extensive, concentrates on California whites to complement the seafood. The list has earned numerous awards and made the Watermark a favorite among local wine connoisseurs. Bottles are attractively displayed in expansive racks behind the bar. **A** startingly incongruous combination of design elements makes for an interesting atmosphere here. Exposed pipes and rafters...the milieu of an historic, 125 year-old warehouse...give customers a sense of yesterday when industry ruled the riverfront. Today's Flats, however, is about friendliness and frivolity; a comfortable playground that knows no season. Whimsical touches at the Watermark, like the sailboat extended sideways over the bar, symbolize the lighthearted mood of today.

Lunch .... Mon.-Fri. 11:30 am-2:30 pm
Dinner .... Sun.-Thurs. 5:30-10 pm;
                         Fri.& Sat. 5:30- Midnight
Brunch .... Sat.& Sun. 11:30 am-3:00 pm
Valet parking available

Hap Gray, co-owner and general manager

Lu
cuisine

The Setting

The setting of Lu Cuisine presents an interesting East-meets-West dichotomy. Armed with a cooking style developed 2,500 years ago in China's coastal province called Shandong, Lu Cuisine offers light, delicate dishes made of only the freshest ingredients and no MSG for the health-conscious diner of the 90's. Reminiscent of China at its most opulent, the restaurant also has an informal, contemporary ambiance. Spectacular dining rooms on two floors enable guests to relax in posh comfort in rosewood chairs at granite tables liberally spaced to permit intimate conversations. Servers are trained to help diners compose a harmonious meal and to assist guests when selecting from the restaurant's comprehensive list of premium imported and domestic wines.

The Cuisine

Given both their English and Chinese names, menu items offer intriguing possibilities. Appetizers include Ginger Mussels, Shrimp & Seaweed Soup and Spring Rolls (fresh vegetables, shrimp and pork tenderloin wrapped in a crisp shell for dipping in mustard sauce). Artistic Lu methods are meticulously applied to extraordinary entrees of beef, pork, chicken and seafood as well as to fresh vegetables. Unfailingly, the contrast of taste, fragrance, color and texture is emphasized. Each dish has a definite personality of its own.

The Proprietors

Proprietors Steiner and Virginia Huang developed a passion for Lu cuisine on extensive researching forays in the far reaches of China. In their educated view, the discriminating diner who has not sampled the cuisine of Shandong has not really experienced Chinese cuisine.

1228 Euclid Avenue
In the historic Halle Building on Playhouse Square
Open for lunch Mon.-Fri. 11:30am - 2pm, Open for dinner Mon.-Sat. 5-10 p.m.
Valet parking available Reservations recommended 241-8488

The Restaurant of China

53

Ralph DiOrio and Denise Marie Fugo, Co-owners

Sammy's

Serving lunch Mon.-Sat. 11:30-2:30

Dinner Mon.-Thurs. 5:30-10
Fri. & Sat. 5:30-midnight

Major credit cards accepted
Valet parking available

1400 West Tenth Street in the Flats

523-5560

In Cleveland, sophisticated dining is defined in one word - Sammy's. All the elements are nurtured in this upscale establishment: chic warehouse setting with a remarkable view...dazzling Seafood Rawbar...discriminating wine list....live jazz...a creative kitchen committed to preparing the finest contemporary American cuisine, splendidly presented.

Sammy's also defines the word success, as witnessed by consistent recognition as the No. 1 choice among Clevelanders, and one of the top restaurants in the country. Sammy's, in fact, is only the second Ohio restaurant to be elected into the Fine Dining Hall of Fame.

The sensual feast begins with the visual. Floor-to-ceiling windows overlook the busy Cuyahoga River and provide an outstanding view of the Flats' skyline. Tall wooden columns and plum-colored ductwork dominate the 19th Century warehouse. Tables, elegantly set with pink napery, beckon.

All this, of course, is but a prelude to the main event, an adventure in nouvelle cuisine.

For openers, the Seafood Rawbar features Gulf shrimp, Alaskan king crab, selections of clams, oysters, mussels, smoked salmon and smoked trout. Landlubbers may choose appetizers such as wild mushroom soup with roasted duck and sage spaetzle or linguini with Italian prosciutto and sauteed eggplant in a fresh tomato sauce.

At least two fresh fish selections are among the entree options every day. Signature entrees include breast of chicken wrapped in phyllo pastry and baked to a golden brown, sauteed medallions of veal, roasted rack of lamb with a pistachio nut coating, and grilled center cut filet of beef. Two unique side dishes accompany each entree.

Wines have been carefully selected for their affinity to the menu. The list of domestic and imported varieties plus an impressive aggregation of champagne and sparkling wines have earned for Sammy's the Wine Spectator Award of Excellence.

This is not the place to equivocate about dessert. Homemade cheesecake, marjolaine with creme anglaise, homemade ice cream and sorbet or Sammy's signature dessert, Boule de Neige, offer a delightful finale to an unforgettable dining experience.

Don's
Pomeroy House

13664 Pearl Rd.. Strongsville **572-1111**

Donald W. Strang and **Donald W. Strang, III,** Proprietors

Those who dine at Don's Pomeroy House are in very good company. This has been a popular gathering place for nearly a century and a half.

The resplendent restaurant, the antithesis of clone-like eateries, was fashioned from an historical residence build on Strongsville Commons in 1847. The home of entrepreneur Alanson Pomeroy became the social center in the town's fledgling days. After meticulous restoration, the Greek Revival classic was honored with a spot on the National Register of Historic Places. Rich woods, Victorian furnishings and genteel framed prints establish the mood.

While this extraordinary setting is impressive, its appeal would fade were it not matched by exceptional cuisine and attentive servers. Not to worry. Food and service are every bit as appealing as the setting.

Snuggling into a deeply upholstered armchair, a guest may sample impeccably fresh fish and seafood. Other excellent entree choices include prime steaks, veal and chicken.

Strang Management Corporation operates two other unique restaurants in the Cleveland area. Also a landmark building, Don's Lighthouse Inn is minutes from downtown at the end of Memorial Shoreway (961-6700). An informal ambiance prevails at Don's River City Cafe, 21290 Center Ridge Rd., near the airport (333-9844).

Considering the popularity of all three establishments, the prudent will want to make reservations.

Lunch served **Dinner:** 5-10 Mon.-Thurs.
5-11 Fri. & Sat.
4-9 Sunday

LEON BIBB

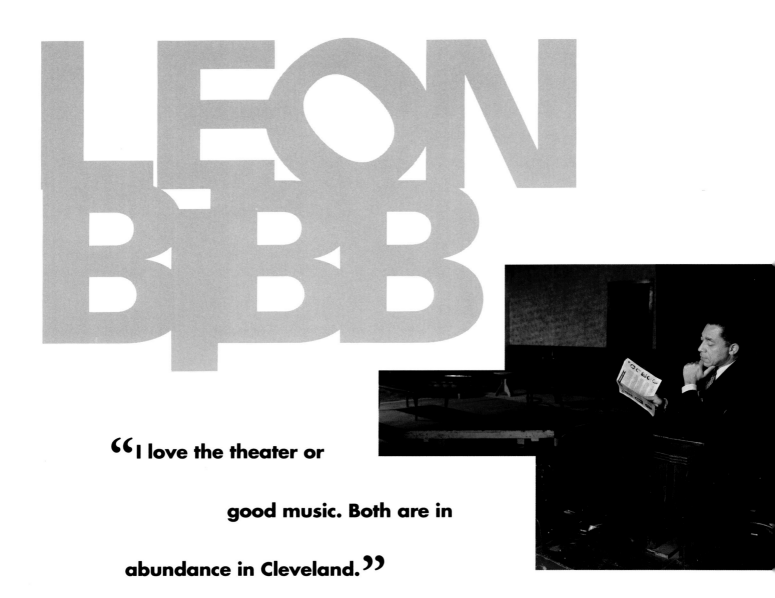

"I love the theater or good music. Both are in abundance in Cleveland."

As one of the city's most active and eloquent citizens, TV 3 news anchor Leon Bibb knows Cleveland well. Given the opportunity to showcase his town over the course of a weekend, Leon would portray a diverse, well-rounded city with offerings to meet all tastes. This charming Clevelander knows of so many sights to see in and around town, that chances are one weekend would never suffice.

Choice selections from the best of Leon's weekend include: dinner along the river in the Flats . . . a performance at Karamu House Theater . . . a walk along the diverse terrain of the Metroparks . . . a tour of University Circle and its many museums . . . a ballgame with either the Indians, Browns, Cavs or Crunch, depending on the season . . . an evening of great music at one of the local colleges . . . Sunday morning church services . . . brunch at a local hotel . . . a walk through The Garden Center of Greater Cleveland and the Cultural Gardens located along Martin Luther King Jr. Drive . . . a performance at The Cleveland Institute of Music or The Cleveland Music School Settlement . . . a visit to the USS Cod, the World War II submarine.

attractions

jaunts

From the

spectacular

to the ordinary,

Cleveland is a city

waiting to

be discovered.

& adventures

Sea World of Ohio
1100 Sea World Drive
Aurora
800/63-SHAMU
216/995-2121

Children will delight in Shamu's Happy

Harbor - new to Sea World in 1992!

By Ann M. Zoller

Make contact with another world at Sea World of Ohio, where you'll find the most comprehensive display of marine life in the midwest.

This beautifully landscaped 90-acre park is a family showplace that is unique to mid-America. Being one of only four in the country, it attracts thousands from throughout the region.

Located 2 miles southeast of Cleveland in Aurora, Sea World of Ohio presents six major shows and more than twenty other attractions including Shamu and Namu, the killer whales, the Penguin Encounter, featuring over 100 penguins, the World of the Sea Aquarium, and champion water skiers.

Shamu's Happy Harbor will add another exciting attraction to the park in 1992. A colorful Caribbean-themed play area with four stories of net climbs, slides, a water maze, a life-size fun ship and many other play elements will delight both kids and adults.

The Sea Monsters and Dinosaurs outdoor display, set in a natural-looking environment, take visitors to another era with exciting life-size animatroncis monsters and dinosaurs.

Your visit to Sea World of Ohio will also feature visits from sea lions, walrus, otters and dolphins in ways you've never imagined.

The Arcade

Galleria at Erieview

down town

The true center of the city is **Public Square.** With the sixty-year-old Terminal Tower as its centerpiece, a once-defunct train station has been transformed into **Tower City Center,** a sleek, glass-encased showpiece of office towers, hotels, and shops. **The Avenue** at Tower City Center encompasses three levels of world-class retail, sophisticated eateries and an 11-screen cinema. 771-0033.

The Arcade, a 100-year-old, five-story colonnade is the largest—and possibly the grandest—in the United States. Glass skylights look down on marble staircases and brass railings in this unique architectural beauty. Today, The Arcade is home to offices, shops and restaurants. 621-8500.

The **Cleveland Public Library** is the largest public library in Northeast Ohio and one of the largest open-shelf libraries in the U.S. with over 6.5 million volumes. The **Eastman Garden** is cloaked between the library's two main buildings. Named in honor of Linda Eastman, Director of the Cleveland Public Library from 1918 - 1938, this idyllic respite is a popular lunchtime escape for many downtown workers. 623-2800.

Dedicated on July 4, 1916, the **Cleveland City Hall** is classically designed in gray granite. The Rotunda or main lobby of the building features the "Spirit of '76" painting by Archibald Willard.

The **Galleria at Erieview,** a glittering, glass shopping plaza features two stories of fine designer shops, restaurants and a food court. Natural sunlight showers the airy, sophisticated mall making any shopping excursion the fun and relaxing diversion it should be. 621-9999.

Cleveland City Hall

Over $11 million dollars was invested in transforming 7.6 lakefront acres, right next to Cleveland's Municipal Stadium, into **North Coast Harbor.** The **William G. Mather Museum** is a new addition to the Harbor, located at the end of the East 9th Street Pier. The 618 foot Great Lakes oar freighter is available for full vessel tours from May through October (574-6262). While at the pier, sightseers may watch the hustle of the largest overseas cargo port on Lake Erie. Visitors to North Coast Harbor in the summer will enjoy the finger-licking fun of many city events at the site. Future plans call for the addition of the Rock 'n' Roll Hall of Fame and Museum, shops, and other tourist attractions.

One of Cleveland's proudest jewels, **Playhouse Square** boasts three magnificently restored 1920 epic theaters in the Ohio, State and Palace theaters. Capacity crowds rise to their feet to applaud the Cleveland Ballet, Great Lakes Theater Festival, Cleveland Opera and visiting performances—from cabaret-style to full-scale Broadway productions. 241-6000.

The **Terminal Tower Observation Deck** affords some of the most spectacular views of the city. Located on the 42nd story of the Terminal Tower, the Observation Deck is open 11:00 a.m. - 4:00 p.m. on weekends and holidays. 621-7981.

The **U.S.S. Cod,** a World War II submarine which survived seven patrols in the South Pacific (some lasted as long as 63 days), is on permanent display at the north end of East 9th Street. No admission is charged, although donations are accepted for the Save the Cod Foundation, which keeps the Cod in Cleveland. 566-8770.

The Flats! Cleveland has developed a new national reputation on the mystique, excitement and distinctive character of this low-lying expanse along the Cuyahoga River. With nearly forty nightclubs, bars and restaurants packed along the teeming riverbanks, the Flats is uniquely designed to accommodate all. On any typical summer weekend, over 120,000 revelers will follow the call to the Flats. The river itself is a hotbed of activity as sailboats, rowing teams and the gaudy powerboat crowd posture for the chance to see and be seen.

The east bank of the Flats offers a potpourri of sensory delights. From the haute cuisine at the posh **Sammy**'s to the boilermaker crowd at **Biggie's Crooked River Saloon,** a stroll down Old River Road is a true adventure. Hot spots include the **Watermark Restaurant,** known for its fresh "sophisticated" seafood, casual elegance and riverfront patio; the **River's Edge,** a beer drinkers delight with an international deli; **Fagan's,** one of the Flats' firsts, and great for the "Happy Hour" crowd; **Aquilon**—Big Band Saturday nights fill the trendy dance floors; the **Flat Iron Cafe,** an Irish pub where longshoremen rub elbows with the young and fashionable.

Nautica, a multi-faceted entertainment complex, encompasses the entire west bank of the Flats. Two imposing jack-knife bridges mark the parameters of the complex as a fitting salute to the industrial roots of the Flats. The **Nautica Stage,** an impressive 4,100-seat, outdoor amphitheater, is perched on the riverbank at the southern tip of the project.

Adjacent to the stage is the recently renovated **Powerhouse,** a dramatic architectural gem which originally powered the city's electric rail system. The exposed brick and expansive atria serve as a gorgeous rustic home to **T.G.I.Friday's;** the **Improv,** the country's best-known laugh house; **Powerplay,** a high-tech gameroom, bar and diner with an emphasis on fun, high-volumed competition; **Grand Slam Grille,** a sports-theme restaurant with memorabilia from the highs and lows in Cleveland sports; **Windows on the River,** a private catering facility; **Howl at the Moon,** a sing-along bar with dueling grand pianos; and many specialty retail shops.

The Powerhouse at Nautica

Further down the half-mile boardwalk is **NRG** ("energy"), a glitzy glass-fronted nightclub, where nightly theatrics inspire one to expect the unexpected. The huge dance floor is a dazzling display of sights and sounds amidst an elegant, high-tech setting.

Next, it's **Jillian's Billiard Club,** a swank, upscale boite with the emphasis on Billiard Club–not pool hall. The decidedly sophisticated club features thirty tables in an opulent setting full of rich woods and designer touches. A casual yet innovative menu makes this stop a different and totally enjoyable diversion.

At the end of the boardwalk is **Shooters Waterfront Cafe U.S.A.** An endless array of powerboats, yachts, poolside posers and wandering tourists make this a prime spot for people watching. An eclectic menu taps all favorites and attracts thousands to this Florida-born hot spot.

far & **Near**

Cleveland's **West Side Market,** which sits at the doorstep of Ohio City, should not be missed. This old-world-style indoor and outdoor market presents a delectable slice of life reminiscent of an earlier era. Over 100 merchants representing virtually all of Cleveland's ethnic pockets peddle fresh produce, meats, cheese and baked goods in dynamic chaos. Open Monday, Wednesday, Friday and Saturday. 781-3663.

Just east of University Circle lies yet another testament to Cleveland's deep ethnic roots. **Little Italy** has preserved the timeless essence of "the neighborhood" as only an authentic Italian community can. Brick streets are rich with tempting aromas and jammed with houses, bistros, bakeries, churches and galleries which make for amusing browsing and excellent eating!

The **NASA Lewis Research Center** is located near Cleveland Hopkins International Airport in Brookpark and displays the history and milestones of space exploration and everyday uses of space technology. Tours of lab facilities and special programs are available by appointment. Other exhibits are open to the public Monday - Sunday. 2100 Brookpark Road. 433-2001.

President James A. Garfield's monument and John D. Rockefeller's grave share a beautiful Eden-like setting at **Lakeview Cemetery** with many other Cleveland history makers. Located at 12316 Euclid Avenue, or enter at the top of Mayfield Road Hill at Kenilworth Road. 421-2665.

Holden Arboretum is a living museum on 2,900 acres of varied terrain, containing 15,000 varieties of trees, shrubs and vines from around the world; six ponds; a sugar maple house and harvesting; wild deer and geese; picnicking, hiking and cross country skiing; a museum; a library; and gift shop in this nature lovers' paradise. Open Tuesday - Sunday. Located at 9500 Sperry Road in Mentor. 946-4400.

Coventry is a unique assortment of coffee houses, outdoor cafes, bistros, exotic little shops and galleries. Cleveland's own Rive Gauche, located at Coventry and Euclid Heights Roads in Cleveland Heights.

For animal lovers, trips around the world depart daily at the **Cleveland Metroparks Zoo,** the tenth oldest in the country. More than 3,000 animals occupy the picturesque beauty of the 165-acre wooded area. 661-7511.

Lawnfield was the home of the 20th President, James A. Garfield. Garfield acquired the house in 1876 and conducted the first successful "front porch" campaign as more than 17,000 people from all over the

Above: The Ledges at Virginia Kendall Park

country came by train to listen to him speak from the porch. Located off I-90 on Rte. 20, off the Rte. 306 exit. 255-8722.

The southwestern shores of Lake Erie, roughly an hour's drive from Cleveland, are commonly referred to as **Wine Country**. There some of the state's finest vineyards produce a variety of award-winning wines. The natural basin-like effect of the lake makes for ideal growing conditions throughout much of the state's northwest region. Tours of wineries are available and many have quaint eateries or restaurants on the grounds making for a delightful excursion. 800/227-6972.

The **Lake Erie Islands** attract thousands of visitors year-round. Located off the northwestern shores of the state, the Islands are but a ferry ride away and offer an unusual conglomeration of sights and sounds which are sure to please. Of the four islands—Kelley's Island, North Bass Island, Middle Bass Island and South Bass Island—the latter is the most popular, known simply as **Put-in-Bay.** Once on the island, bicycle and golf cart rentals simplify the abundant opportunities for sightseeing. Of historical significance is **Perry's Monument,** commemorating the end of the War of 1812 which followed a dramatic victory in the Battle of Lake Erie. Tours of the island and its local wineries, quaint shops, a variety of restaurants, pubs, festivals and an active boating population make this getaway an ideal escape.

Several local companies offer guided tours of the Cleveland area. **Trolley Tours of Cleveland** offers sleekly designed trolleys which may be used as full tour packages or simply as inspired transportation. 771-4484.

The **Goodtime III** offers river and lake cruises which are both informative and fun. 861-5110.

Northeast Ohio is in the enviable position of having three major amusement parks located within a reasonable driving distance. Sea World of Ohio, Geagua Lake and Cedar Point Amusement Park are all national attractions within easy reach of the Cleveland market.

Sea World of Ohio is a great family adventure which is both highly entertaining and educational. Children and adults of all ages will love the feature shows, educational exhibits and attractions which foster understanding and appreciation of marine animals. 800/63-SHAMU.

Neighboring **Geagua Lake** has more than 100 rides and attractions, including Turtle Beach's Totally Expanded Kid-Kontrolled Amphibious Action Area for children. Other features include 4 roller coasters, the Wave, live shows and restaurants. 800/THE-WAVE.

One hour west of Cleveland is **Cedar Point Amusement Park.** The world's tallest and fastest roller coaster, the $7.5 million Mean Streak, is one of the record-breaking 10 roller coasters and sixty rides in the 164-acre park. 419/626-0830.

International Exposition Center

One of Cleveland's most important landmarks is also a world renowned venue for entertainment and special events. The International Exposition Center, adjacent to Cleveland Hopkins International Airport, is listed in the **Guinness Book of World Records** as the world's largest single-building exposition facility.

With 2.5 million square feet under its roof, the I-X Center can accommodate nearly every event imaginable: conventions, trade shows, exhibitions, parties, banquets, sporting events, concerts . . . and the world's largest indoor amusement park.

Over 2 million visitors are attracted to the I-X Center annually. Among the Center's most popular annual public shows are the I-X Center Indoor Amusement Park, the Greater Cleveland Auto Show, the Mid-America Boat Show, The Annual American & Canadian Sports, Travel & Outdoor Show and the National Home & Garden Show.

For year-round fun the I-X Center has added a permanent indoor Ferris wheel—the largest indoor gondola wheel in the world. Some 35 feet of the I-X Ferris Wheel soars above the roof in a glass enclosure, offering riders breathtaking views of the airport and Cleveland's downtown skyline.

"The I-X Amusement Park brings all the sights and sounds of summer indoors for an entire month each spring, with a 20-acre midway of high-speed rides, a Giant Kiddieland and special attractions," Patrick M. Park, president, I-X Center.

Each April the I-X Center hosts the world's largest indoor amusement park. For year-round fun, the I-X Center offers a 10-story indoor Ferris Wheel.

The Mid-America Boat Show is the largest indoor boat and fishing show in the country with over 1,000 sail and power boats on display. The Greater Cleveland Auto Show is one of the nation's largest auto shows with displays from over 40 manufacturers of new cars, vans and trucks. The Annual American & Canadian Sports, Travel & Outdoor Show is America's largest sports show, covering 16 acres with over 2,000 booths and displays of fishing and camping equipment, travel information, hot air balloons, boats and RVs.

In addition to these record-setting events, the Business & Industry Show, held May 19 - 21, 1992, is the region's most expansive business show of its type, with both national and international exhibitors.

The I-X Center has welcomed Presidents Carter, Reagan and Bush in recent years, all of whom have landed at the I-X Jet Center, the I-X Center's own luxurious private air terminal. The newly-renovated Jet Center features 500,000 sq. ft. of ramp area, 70,000 sq. ft. of heated and recently refurbished hangers and 20,000 sq. ft. of office space and a pilot's lounge. The I-X Jet Center is the largest fixed base operation (FBO) in Cleveland.

6200 Riverside Drive
Adjacent to
Cleveland Hopkins
International Airport
676-6000

Weather, Woollybears and **Dick Goddard**. You just can't have one without the other in Cleveland. As the Newscenter 8 meteorologist, Dick Goddard *is* weather in Cleveland. Generations of Clevelanders have come to appreciate Dick's down-home style and his always interesting asides and anecdotes. Dick's three-day forecast for fun is guaranteed to brighten up any weekend excursion.

Highlights of the weekend: dinner at Celebrities **sports restaurant in Independence . . . the** Lake Erie Nature and Science Center **. . . delectable ethnic delights at** Parma Perogis **restaurant . . .** The Cleveland Museum of Natural History **. . . the** Music Box Haus **in Vermilion, where hundreds of dolls are displayed . . . laughs at** Hilarities Comedy Club **. . .** Sfuzzi's **trendy Italian cuisine . . . woollybear gathering . . . brunch at** Stouffer Tower City Plaza Hotel **. . . a trip to the** Cleveland Metroparks Zoo **. . . dinner at the** Panorama Restaurant **in Westlake.**

"This weekend is designed to show-case some of my favorite Cleveland spots."

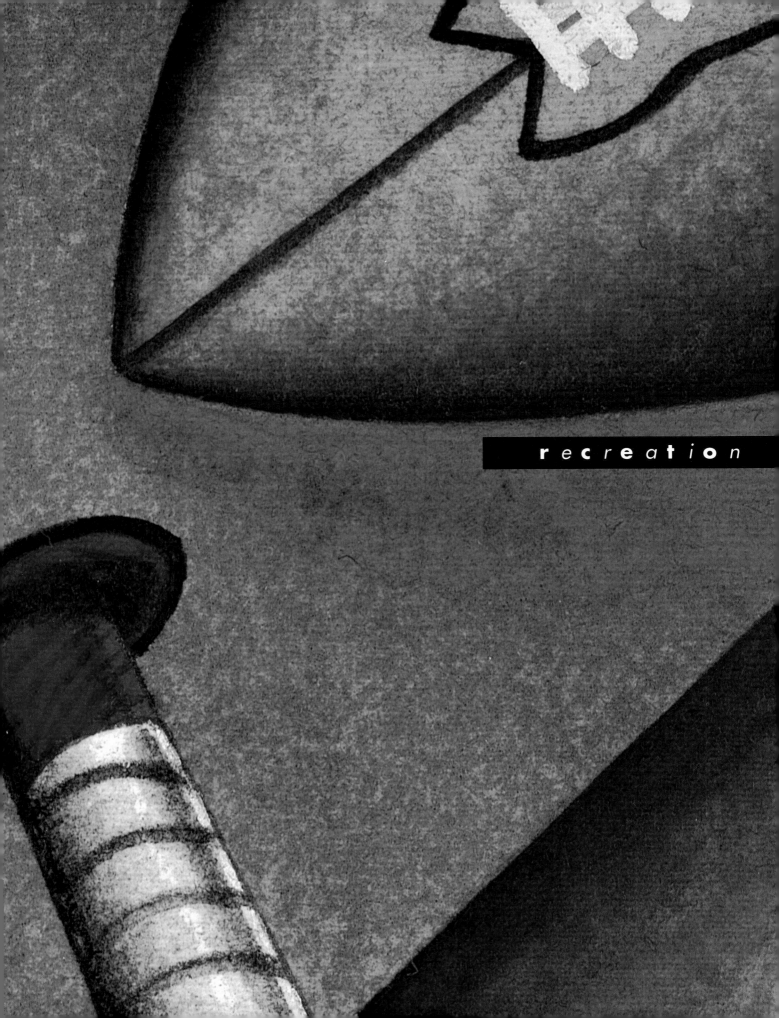

recreation

athletic

Here in Cleveland, **sports fanaticism** is nearly epidemic. Cleveland plays in the big leagues, with franchises in every major professional sport: the Cleveland **Indians** (American League baseball), the Cleveland **Browns** (National Football League), the Cleveland **Cavaliers** (National Basketball Association), and the Cleveland **Crunch** (Major Soccer League).

diversions

Those wishing to take a **more active role** in sports are also in **an enviable situation.** Cleveland is **noteworthy** for having an abundance of facilities where **athletic pursuits**—both indoor and outdoor—can be aggressively pursued.

By Van McCulloch

escape

the big leagues Major league sports, of course, attract the largest, most passionate crowds. The venerable **Municipal Stadium** stands tall among our country's traditional fields of competition - a symbol of Cleveland's historic role in professional sports. With seating for 80,000, it is also among the largest in the United States. The stadium's heyday may be waning, as plans for the Gateway stadium and arena complex move forward. However, despite any and all future sports complex developments in Cleveland—the legacy of Municipal Stadium will endure, having been carefully etched in Cleveland's proud athletic history.

the metropolitan maelstrom

and find

Wherever games are played, or whatever the team's fortunes, Clevelanders remain devoutly loyal to the **Cleveland Indians**–"the Tribe"– one of only three charter teams left in the American League.

Passion for the **Cleveland Browns** is equally fervent. The team has enjoyed one of the NFL's proudest pasts and has spent many a season among the league's elite. Browns mania grips all of Northeast Ohio during football season, as Cleveland fans are known for being some of the most zealous in the league. Despite the often frigid winds whipping off the lake and swirling around Municipal Stadium, it is a rare occasion when all 80,000 seats are not crammed, in an avid sea of brown and orange. The Browns have been a major factor in Cleveland for more than 40 years, and have graduated a dozen superstars to the Pro Football Hall of Fame, located in nearby Canton, Ohio.

the respite and renewal

of greenspace

For the all the gravity-defying thrills of the NBA, look no farther than the **Cleveland Cavaliers.** The heart-stopping action of the Cavs has kept basketball fans on their feet at the Richfield Coliseum for years. Also doing battle at the Coliseum, the **Cleveland Crunch** is the city's newest professional team. The booming popularity of the sport is breeding a whole generation of devoted young fans.

Above: Sanctuary Marsh at North Chagrin Reservation

While Cleveland's status as a
mecca for professional teams is almost without peer,
the variety of other spectator sports is also exceptional. Turf fans
cheer on their favorite thoroughbreds at **Thistledown Race Track** or enjoy
harness racing at **Northfield Park.** The nation's oldest air show, the **Cleveland
National Air Show,** is also held at Burke Lakefront Airport on Labor Day
weekend. **playing in the parks** Cleveland is also a haven for nature
lovers. Newcomers to the city are astonished to learn that they can escape the metropolitan maelstrom
and find the respite and renewal of greenspace within 15 minutes of anywhere in Cleveland. **T**his enviable
urban park system, the **Cleveland Metroparks,** includes 18,000 acres of unspoiled woodland stretching
from the North Chagrin Reservation on the east to Rocky River on the west side. Along with the Metroparks
Zoo, this "Emerald Necklace" encircles the city on three sides. More than 80 miles of scenic park roadways con-
nect the 12 parks known as "reservations." **V**ariety is the watchword in this expanse of natural beauty. Wildlife
and waterfowl find sanctuary among hiking, biking and bridle trails. There are picnic areas and nature centers. Golf
courses and playfields. Lakes for fishing, swimming and boating. Cross-country ski trails, hills for sledding and refriger-
ated chutes for tobogganing. There is even a photography club. Five Nature Centers provide visitors information
and entertainment. **A**t the South Chagrin Reservation is the **Metropolitan Polo Field,** headquarters of the
Cleveland Polo Club. The venerable sport is enjoying a renaissance in this country, and fans champion their favorite
teams at matches held on Sunday afternoons. The field is also used by dog clubs and for horse shows, including the
prestigious **Hunter-Jumper Classic,** highlight of the oldest equestrian Grand Prix in America. **hitting
the links** Cleveland Metroparks operate six public golf courses, ranging from a par three and an executive course to championship layouts that challenge even the best of golfers. Three of them: Big Met, Little Met and
Mastick Woods, are located in Rocky River Reservation. Sleepy Hollow is in Brecksville, Shawnee Hills in
Bedford and Manakiki, the championship course (a real challenge!), is located in Willoughby Hills. From mid-
March through mid-November, the courses are open daily from dawn to dusk. **T**he six are among an
astonishing number of public and private courses in the area. Nearly 3,000 courses beautify the
Northern Ohio landscape where the natural mix of rolling hills, flat expanses and verdant forests is
the stuff of dreams for a golf course architect. **W**hile the profusion of courses is remark-
able, there is good reason: avid interest in the sport is par for the course as
Clevelanders spend more money on golf, per capita, than do residents of any
other city in the country. **g**olf is also a spectator sport here.
Numerous PGA tournaments are staged in Northern
Ohio, including the NEC World Series of

Golf and the Ameritech Senior Open. Regional PGA organizations also sponsor opens for their member pros, tournaments that customarily offer a free opportunity to study the techniques of non-celebrity pros.

Water Sports For the sportive Clevelander, the city provides the best of both worlds. Opportunities for water sports are every bit as abundant as the options for the landlubber.

Lakefront State Park comprises the separate entities of Edgewater, Euclid Beach, Gordon and Wildwood parks and the E. 55th Street Marina. This extravagant shoreline draws thousands of sun worshippers, yachtsmen, swimmers, beach combers and fishermen eager to land a prized walleye.

Cleveland is also an apt location for sailing events such as the **Star Class World's Championship** and various powerboat races. **Cleveland Race Week** features competitions for both sailboats and powerboats.

Members of the **Flats Racing League** enjoy the growing sport of sculling, dipping their oars with precision as they sweep past bistros lining the Cuyahoga River's famous Flats entertainment district. Also in the Flats, at the Nautica entertainment complex, **The Boat Club** offers boating instruction and access to powerboats and sailboats ranging from 28 to 70 feet in length.

The Angler's Angle While living on Lake Erie is reason enough to hang out the Gone Fishin' sign, Cleveland anglers are also tempted by rivers stocked with salmon and trout.

The lake offers an abundance of perch and is famous for being "The Walleye Capitol of the World." The Ohio Department of Natural Resources says there are 100 fishing "hot spots" near Cleveland…in breakwaters, jetties and channels…in coves and estuaries…near points and spits…and in the Lake Erie Island region as well.

Stream fishing in the Chagrin and Rocky rivers yields coho and chinook salmon, rainbow trout, channel catfish. Smaller lakes have excellent bluegill, large and small mouth bass, crappie and some rainbow trout. There are nine fishing areas in the Metroparks alone. The same lakes, ponds and streams that provide warm weather enjoyment furnish sporting pleasure for ice fisherman when snow blankets the countryside.

I-90 at Route 44, exit 200
Concord
352-6201
800/792-0258

quail hollow

A Club Resort

Quail Hollow has hosted a number of major tournaments, including United States Amateur Qualifiers, the Ohio Open, The Ben Hogan Cleveland Open, and the Northern Ohio PGA Sectional Championship.

One area golf course, Quail Hollow, has hosted a number of major tournaments, including United States Amateur Qualifiers, the Ohio Open, The Ben Hogan Cleveland Open, and the Northern Ohio PGA Sectional Championship. Located nearby in Concord, Quail Hollow is an 18-hole, par-72 championship course designed by Bruce Devlin who now competes on the PGA Senior Tour.

Quail Hollow, a Club Resort, is also a prime example of a phenomenal development: the weekend golf getaway. Former golf "widows" and "orphaned" children may now accompany the fairway fanatic for a fun-filled weekend at a resort that caters to both the player and the non-golfer. Quail Hollow also accommodates weekend business meetings and retreats on a year-round basis.

Whatever the season, Quail Hollow has recreational opportunities aplenty, such as tennis, swimming, jogging, a health spa and cross-country skiing. Quail Hollow also provides posh accommodations, dining, entertainment and a fully-equipped conference center.

This posh recreational resort accommodates

weekend business retreats on a year-round basis

MARY ROSE OAKAR

"With so much to see and do in Cleveland, I try to show visitors the diversity of the city."

Naturally, Congresswoman Mary Rose Oakar can't spend all her time in Cleveland. But when she does, she knows where to go and what to do to immerse herself in that good old Cleveland frame of mind. We asked Congresswoman Oakar what city sights she would showcase to a convention selection committee or business executives not familiar with Cleveland. The results are a perfect recipe for mixing business with pleasure.

Highlights of the weekend: dinner at Massimo da Milano . . . an evening of jazz at Club Isabella . . . a down-home breakfast at Billy's and browsing along Antique Row on Lorain Avenue . . . lunch at the old-world West Side Market . . . the Top of the Town restaurant for dinner . . . a performance at Playhouse Square . . . brunch at Heck's Cafe in Ohio City . . . the Center for Contemporary Art and The Cleveland Museum of Art . . . a boating excursion on the lake . . . dinner at Jim's Steak House.

"There is no comparison to a winning effort at the stadium in front of 80,000."

BERNIE KOSAR

Growing up in nearby Youngstown Ohio, Bernie Kosar always dreamed of playing for the Cleveland Browns. Having realized that dream as quarterback, Bernie has become a true hometown hero. And while he sees plenty of action on the field, Bernie and his wife Babette like things a little more relaxed when looking for a fun weekend in Cleveland.

Bernie's gameplan for weekend fun includes: dinner at the Grand Slam Grille restaurant followed by some friendly but heated competition at Powerplay, the high-tech gameroom located in the Powerhouse . . . a day of golfing, preparing for the Bernie Kosar Charity Classic at Tanglewood Country Club . . . dinner at Heck's Restaurant in Rocky River . . . a family picnic in the Metroparks.

business

for even more dramatic growth in the 90s.

The comeback city of the 80s is poised

The BP America Building at Public Square

IMPRESSIVE
B U S I N E S S   A D D R E S S

Cleveland received much acclaim in the 1980s for its well documented turnaround. Over the course of a single decade, this city wrestled itself from the grips of default and wrote an innovative script for its own dramatic success story. From industrial giant, to rust belt decline to a rejuvenated, restructured economic base, Cleveland has come full circle.

Though it was hard to remember during the dark days of the seventies, Cleveland's proud past is primarily a tale of prosperity and growth. Throughout the latter half of the nineteenth century, Cleveland began to assume its place as a thriving metropolitan city, home to such industrial giants as John D. Rockefeller, founder of the Standard Oil of Ohio Company and Marcus A. Hanna of the M.A. Hanna Company. With steel and heavy industry providing a solid foundation, Cleveland continued to be one of the nation's powerhouses as it entered the 1900s. It remained a productive, growing center through much of the century, benefitting from the industrial demands of the World Wars as well as the post World War II economic boom. As the market for steel declined in the '70s, so too did Cleveland's economy. Like many major northeastern cities, Cleveland was slow to respond to a changing economy and fell victim to the plague of the rustbelt. The bottom fell out in 1979, as Cleveland suffered the sobering reality of default. Seeing nowhere to go but up, the corporate and political communities formed an uncommon alliance and began to rally the economy.

By Ann M. Zoller

Slowly and deliberately, the economic base in Cleveland has shifted from heavy industry to a more stable mix, which relies heavily on service and health care. This newfound economic health, along with a greatly improved infrastructure, has attracted new businesses and an impressive array of developments.

All of this points to a balanced and productive future for Northeast Ohio.

Over $5-billion of development is currently in process or slated to take place. Cleveland is home to two of the nation's top five developers, Forest City Enterprises, Inc. and The Richard & David Jacobs Group. Both companies were able to concentrate efforts on their hometown by taking advantage of opportunities offered by Cleveland's impressive new business climate.

The Richard & David Jacobs Group completed downtown's first upscale retail complex with the Galleria and Towers at Erieview in 1987. In addition, the company recently changed the face of downtown's central Public Square with the construction of what is the tallest building in Ohio with the 57-story Society Center and 400-room Marriott hotel on the northeast quadrant.

Forest City Enterprises, Inc. has completed the first phase of its mammoth Tower City Center project. One of the largest mixed-use developments in the country, the Center currently includes a refurbished Terminal Tower office building; a glass-encased mall featuring three stories of shops, restaurants and downtown's only cineplex; two new office towers, the 14-story Ritz-

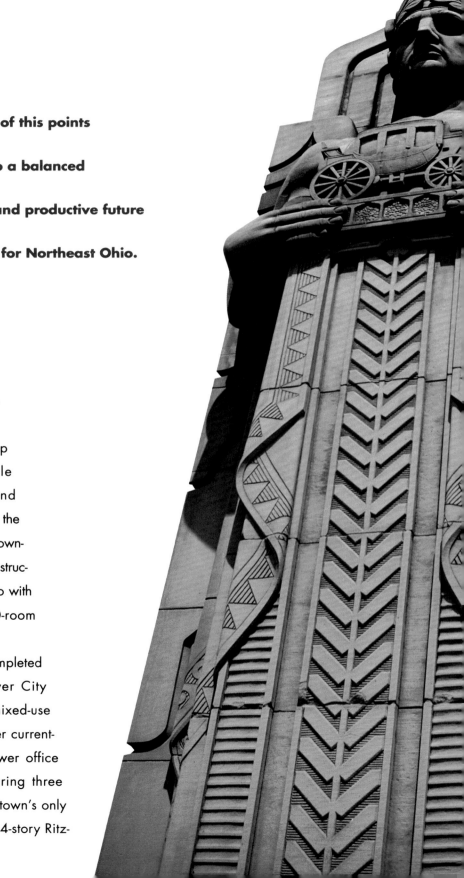

Hope Memorial Bridge

Carlton Hotel and Office Tower and the 12-story Skylight Office Tower; and downtown's only rail transit station, which recently completed a $5 million state-of-the-art renovation. Connected to Tower City Center is the Stouffer Tower City Plaza Hotel which has recently completed its own massive $37-million renovation.

Other recent developments include the spectacular North Point Tower, the 28-story Bank One Center, the striking Renaissance on Playhouse Square office tower and the Nautica entertainment complex in the area known as the Flats along the Cuyahoga River.

The surge in development has been complemented by an influx of new companies relocating to the area, giving Cleveland the fourth highest concentration of Fortune 500 industrial headquarters. These include Goodyear Tire & Rubber Co., TRW, Inc., Eaton Corp., Parker Hannifin Corp., B.F. Goodrich, Sherwin-Williams Co., Gen-Corp, Inc., Reliance Electric, Lubrizol Corp., NACCO Industries, Inc., Figgie International, Inc., American Greetings Corp., Ferro Corp., M.A. Hanna Co., Lincoln-Electric, A. Schulman, Inc., Standard Products Co., and Sealy Holdings.

Enterprises already located in Cleveland, as well as those eyeing a move to the comeback city, are served by the Greater Cleveland Growth Association, the local chamber of commerce. The association's mission encompasses three major program areas: community betterment, job creation and direct service to members.

Soon to celebrate its 150th anniversary, the Growth Association is one of the oldest and most respected chambers of commerce in America. In 1990 its membership topped 10,000 companies, making it the largest metropolitan chamber of commerce in the country's history.

In Cleveland's new economic base, manufacturing has shifted from 31 percent to under 23 percent of employment. Research and development, the polymer industry and some of the country's finest health care facilities are strong up-and-comers. There is the sustaining strength of well established legal and financial companies. Growth in the service industries is increasing. All of this points to a balanced and productive future for northeast Ohio.

Our New Marriott Is Helping Redefine What Is Meant By Greater Cleveland.

Greater Cleveland now means a city with lots of exciting, dramatic changes.

In fact, over $5 billion worth. Like the North Coast Harbor for recreation, the Galleria for shopping, the Flats for nightlife and the new Marriott Society Center for your next business trip or group meeting.

You'll not only be in the heart of it all, but directly across from the Convention Center as well.

And you'll love our changes as much as Cleveland's. Including the most flexible meeting space downtown, all on the first floor. Plus, the beauty of a contemporary art deco decor. As well as the convenience of two phones with computer and fax hook-ups in your room.

There's also Marriott's Honored Guest Awards,® the richest awards program in the business. Not to mention the incomparable service that's made Marriott famous.

So come to downtown Cleveland's most distinctive hotel. Where changes are taking place for the better.

CLEVELAND
Marriott®
SOCIETY CENTER

SERVICE. THE ULTIMATE LUXURY.®

127 Public Square, Cleveland, OH 44114-1305
Call us direct (216) 696-9200, your travel professional, or call toll-free, 1-800-228-9290.

FRED LINDA

As the ever-congenial host of The Morning Exchange **on TV 5, Fred Griffith has been helping Clevelanders jumpstart their mornings for years. With wife Linda, the twosome are known as the area's most noted gourmets, having authored two cook books together,** The Best of the Midwest **and** Grown in the U.S.A. **Their weekend recipe for fun is sure to please even the most discriminating palate.**

Highlights of the weekend include: a taste-testing extravaganza at the Baricelli Inn **. . . a walking tour of** Wade Lagoon **and the** Severance Hall **area around** University Circle **. . . a visit to** The Cleveland Museum of Art **including a delicious snack at** The Museum Cafe **. . . a concert by** The Cleveland Orchestra **at** Severance Hall **. . . a light and jazzy post-concert snack at** Club Isabella **. . . a workout at the** One-to-One Fitness Center **at University Hospitals.**

"The wealth of offerings available in University Circle is truly incredible."

"Although every season is exciting when you're Mary, Mary – Autumn is my favorite."

MARY STRASSMEYER

Everybody but everybody knows Mary, Mary. The Plain Dealer's heralded society columnist virtually defines 'who's who' in Cleveland. Perhaps more than any other single person, Mary Strassmeyer **knows who and what is happening. And with her hand firmly planted on the pulse of the city, who could be better than this native Clevelander to carve out the perfect autumnal weekend.**

Highlights of Mary, Mary's very, very exciting weekend include: dinner at Johnny's Restaurant **on Fulton Road . . . a tour of the ethnic Italian neighborhood around** St. Rocco Church **. . . A jaunt to the** Flats' **famed watering holes . . . shopping at** Tower City Center **and the** Galleria **. . . lunch at** Eddie Khouri's Middle East Restaurant **. . . sightseeing among the city's most elegant suburbs –** Shaker Heights, Gates Mills, Hunting Valley, **and** Chagrin River Road **. . . haute cuisine on the river at** Sammy's **. . . a show at the** Great Lakes Theater Festival **. . . brunch at** Miracles **in Tremont . . . a midday trip to** Hale Farm and Village **. . . dinner at** Morton's Steak House **at** Tower City Center.

lifestyles

Cleveland is a coastal city. This seemingly obvious statement of fact changed forever the life of the city which finally grew to understand its import. Uncovering the wonders of **lakefront living** over the last decade has transformed Cleveland. We've become the **North Coast.** Just as we are realizing the potential offered by our beautiful waterfront environs, Clevelanders are learning to appreciate the countless other attributes we take for granted. From the glory of the four seasons, to the excellent interstate system which allows easy access throughout the city, to the abundance of impressive, affordable housing, to the **envious quality of life** afforded by cultural institutions, extensive park systems and superior schools—Cleveland is very livable.

As a matter of fact, Cleveland is a great place to live. It's a place where families are raised and traditions are born. **Cleveland is home.**

Uncovering the wonders of lakefront living has transformed Cleveland.

By Ann M. Zoller

The Lake

With a prime location on **Lake Erie,** Clevelanders share in a unique resource. As the shallowest of the Great Lakes, Lake Erie stays warmer longer which has a direct effect on the climate of the surrounding land, the huge fish population and **recreational activities.**

Clearly, Cleveland's status as a waterfront community is one of its greatest assets. Remarkably, it could almost be

Great

considered a fresh, new-found attraction. In the past decade, Clevelanders have **rediscovered** the wonders of the water and recreational industries continue to grow, reflecting this boom.

Living on a **Great Lake**

Climate

Surprisingly, many Clevelanders will cite the climate of the city as one of the area's most appealing qualities. The splendor of the **changing seasons** is not something most would give up for a year of any monochromatic climate.

The constant changing of the seasons keeps the city interesting and the senses alert. Life flows in a natural yet distinct calendar. **Seasonal rituals** become traditions which enrich lives and become engrained into memory, ultimately defining life in Cleveland.

Communities

Cleveland offers an abundance of beautiful neighborhoods and residential communities. Lavish tudor estates, breathtaking lakefront vistas and quaintly detailed century homes are just a few of the options available in Cleveland's vast housing market. A growing **string of suburbs** encircles the city, most of which are within twenty miles of downtown via a well-developed freeway system. The average commute in Cleveland is only 23 minutes, which is an enviable benefit for a metropolitan city of Cleveland's size.

Eastern Suburbs

Cleveland Heights is a sophisticated city with a multitude of housing alternatives—from the luxurious to the comfortably affordable. Proximity to universities, hospitals, museums and other cultural attractions gives a **unique urban atmosphere** amidst the conveniences of a well-heeled suburb. Extensive park lands, recreational programs and one of the highest rated school systems in Ohio are significant attractions. The city boasts eight neighborhood shopping areas, specialty shops and fine dining—making Cleveland Heights one of the most active, thriving communities in Cleveland.

Shaker Heights

is one of Cleveland's most distinctive communities. This sophisticated suburb remains among the nation's finest with superior schools, outstanding city services and magnificent homes. A planned community, with homes ranging from $60,000 - $600,000 or more, Shaker Heights' enduring **commitment to quality** is ever-present. Exquisite Tudor estates featuring timeless craftmanship and intricate detail are a testament to the tradition of excellence found in Shaker Heights. Meeting those same high standards are the area's fine Georgian and Colonial homes, two-family rentals, apartments and condominiums. The natural beauty of the area's lush green lands and the sparkling Shaker Lakes leave an imprint of the country in the heart of this residential city.

**City of Shaker Heights
491-1400**

Exquisite Tudor estates featuring timeless craftsmanship and intricate detail are a testament to the tradition of excellence found in Shaker Heights.

Shaker Heights is comprised of people who share common values—the importance of family, home and community—and the lifestyle of this vital, thriving city reflects these priorities. **Excellence in education** is a community-wide commitment as residents take pride in their nationally recognized school system. Leisure activities are plentiful and the club-like setting of Thornton Park offers swimming, tennis and year-round ice skating. The proximity to downtown is an important advantage for the well-educated and accomplished residents of this community and is accentuated by the rapid transit, which transports commuters both downtown and to the airport.

Shaker Heights offers an active relocation program for those interested in moving to the area. City staff members offer personalized tours of the city, schools and recreation facilities free of charge and work with realtors to meet individual needs. For a tour, general information or to explore housing options, contact the City of Shaker Heights at 491-1400.

Beachwood

is one of Cleveland's wealthier suburbs and one of its finest. Beautiful contemporary homes, extensive **recreational amenities** and an excellent school system make this suburb a superior choice. Shoppers from throughout the Cleveland area enjoy the fine offerings of Beachwood Place and the distinctive boutiques of La Place.

Chagrin Falls

has successfully captured the feel of an authentic New England town. Lovely century homes, quaint stops and the cascading falls for which the community is named create a **picture-perfect small town** setting. Visitors from throughout the area flock to boutique-lined Main Street to enjoy the breathtaking scenery and browse among the delightful shops.

Bratenahl

occupies just one square mile on the shores of Lake Erie just east of downtown Cleveland. This **luxurious hideaway** features some of the most gorgeous estates in the country, as well as lavish condominiums and apartments.

Pepper Pike is an ideal community for families.

Large two-story homes sit on **ample wooded lots** in a serene suburban environment. An excellent school system, recreational facilities and proximity to the Metroparks make Pepper Pike one of Cleveland's most desirable locations. The convenience of close-to-home shopping is found at Landerwood Plaza in this primarily residential community.

Solon is located on the far southeastern arm

of the city and is one of the **fastest growing** areas in the region. A wide selection of better living options are offered within this rural city, which is conveniently located off the interstate and in easy distance of many shopping centers.

Gates Mills offers one of Cleve-

land's most beautiful and refined residential alternatives. Lovely estates, including many century homes, are the hallmark of this captivating village. The flowing Chagrin River helps define the balance between **elegant living** and spectacular country comforts.

Cleveland offers an abundance

of beautiful neighborhoods

and residential communities.

Hunting Valley is an exclusive

sanctuary for many of area's elite. Luxurious homes on ample wooded lots are the standard in this very **private community** of gracious estate living. Daisy Hill and Roundwood Manor remain as legacies of Cleveland's famed Van Sweringen brothers. The Daisy Hill Green House is the only facet open to the public.

Moreland Hills is another

fashionable rural retreat on Cleveland's east side. This elegant residential village defines **stately** country living among lush wooded hills. The Garfield Memorial marks the town's center at the Moreland Hills Village Hall.

Hudson is an **historic suburb** located

to the east. A charming town center bustles with activity, as neatly groomed parks and the landmark Clocktower form the backdrop for comfortable **neighborhood shops** and many businesses. **Century homes** compliment the many expansive new developments in Hudson. Top rated public and private schools offer excellent **educational options.** This tightly-knit community takes pride in its family feel, making Hudson an appealing place to call home.

Western Suburbs

Lakewood boasts an extensive range of

housing options from its "Gold Coast" lakefront apartments and condominiums to its **tree-lined streets** of duplex century homes. An enticing array of antique shops make for enjoyable weekend browsing. Lakewood Park is a center of activity, with children at play and free outdoor band concerts held throughout summer months. The excellent services, fine school system, proximity to downtown and **neighborly feel** of this community make Lakewood an attractive choice for many families.

Rocky River is another **charming** suburban retreat along the lake. Classic, understated homes line comfortable wooded streets in this traditional suburban community. Residents enjoy the convenience of nearby Westgate Mall, the upscale flair of Beachcliff Mall and many **specialty shops** located throughout the town's center. The winding Rocky River for which the city is named, and its perch on the Metroparks' valley make Rocky River a beautiful residential option. **Bay Village** is a small, **picturesque community** tucked neatly at the westernmost edge of the county. Huntington Beach, the Lake Erie Nature and Science Center, and Huntington Playhouse are just some of the many attractions which offer activities for families and guests. Of **historical significance** are Rosehill Museum and Cahoon Memorial Rose Garden, which mark the site of the city founders' original homestead. Residents live in traditional Cape Cod and Colonial homes, as well as impressive contemporary homes, which sit on freshly manicured lawns along beautifully tended streets. **Superior schools** and services and a dedication to family make Bay Village one of Cleveland's best offerings. **Westlake** is a **comfortable** upper-middle class suburb which continues to develop at a rapid pace. Many large new developments featuring both classic Georgian and Cape Cod architecture have sprung up in recent years with many more slated for the future. Residents enjoy the benefits of several retail centers

including Williamsburg Square, King James Plaza and Kensington Square. Clague Park draws animal and nature lovers from throughout the area to its delightfully populated duck ponds. **Parma** is the most heavily populated suburb in Cleveland. Neatly kept, affordable housing, a wide array of shopping options, including the expansive Parmatown mall, fine schools, recreational activities, several parks and a **unique ethnic flair** make Parma very livable. **Brecksville** is another rapidly growing suburb. An expansive **revitalization** and renovation program downtown has left its mark on the Brecksville Town Centre with several new boutiques and **retail marts.** A popular choice for professionals due to its handsomely wooded lots, Brecksville is a town built to attract **families.** Ample recreational and social opportunities abound with a municipally owned lake and park area and a new community center planned.

Strongsville is the largest suburban community in Cuyahoga County. A tremendous growth spurt between 1970-1980 made it one of the fastest growing urban areas in the state. And growth continues in this ideal regional setting where the ambience of the country is intertwined with the modern efficiency of the most contemporary **new developments**. A commitment to achieving a healthy balance between the rambling park lands and running rivers and the increasing residential population will continue to attract new families to Strongsville.

Executive Caterers

Executive Caterers has hosted many of Cleveland's finest events over the past thirty years. Headquartered on the grounds of luxurious Landerhaven in Mayfield Heights, Executive Caterers serves over 300,000 people annually. **Set on beautifully manicured and landscaped grounds,** the spectacular Landerhaven offers the finest indoor and outdoor accommodations for all types of events from weddings to corporate trade shows and stockholder dinners. Off-premise catering is offered at numerous sites of choice statewide and beyond.

Committed to responsive management, superior service and outstanding cuisine, Executive Caterers offers fine catering and **elegant accommodations** for your personal or professional needs. An experienced staff works personally with each client to ensure that all details are covered for a **successful event.**

From the Budweiser Cleveland Grand Prix to the Presidential Debates, Executive Caterers serves the community as one of the premier names in the catering industry and the largest catering employer throughout the state.

Executive Caterers at Landerhaven
6111 Landerhaven Drive
Mayfield Heights
449-0700

Realty One is a full-service real estate company which has experienced tremendous success and phenomenal growth within the Northern Ohio market over the last decade. As the seventh largest independent real estate company in the country, the company has **46 residential offices** serving 20 counties. Residential and commercial sales, property management, new-home sales, nationwide relocation and home warranty protection are all offered by Realty One's expert team of experienced professionals.

A sophisticated management style is a big part of Realty One's **dramatic success story.** With over 1,500 active sales associates and 350 employees, the company encourages open communication within a family atmosphere to foster individual and corporate advancement. The Realty One staff is equipped with the newest technological equipment to assure fast and accurate assistance. Quality service is the mainstay of success at Realty One.

**Realty One Corporate Center
6000 Rockside Woods Boulevard
328-2500**

As the seventh largest **Independent realty company in the country, the company has** 46 residential realty offices serving **20 counties.**

"Realty One has invested in Cleveland because we believe in Cleveland, and we haven't been wrong!" Joseph T. Aveni, chairman of the board and chief executive officer.

REALTY ON

One's steadfast commitment to the community.

Corporate Relocation is one of Realty One's most successful divisions. As the winner of the "Overall Broker of the Year" award, the highest honor in America's premier relocation network, Realty One Corporate Relocation is a proven leader in the field. A complex system of people, programs and professionalism ease the problems often accompanying a major transition. From the sophisticated, high-tech SchoolMatch program, which ranks prospective school systems on a regional and national basis, to the **caring personalized service** of the staff, Realty One Corporate Relocation is a must for anyone moving to a new community.

Realty One Corporate Relocation
Terminal Tower, Suite 1415
50 Public Square
523-1800

Pat Mead (front, center) and her Corporate Relocation staff

Kopf Builders
Cleveland's Relocation Specialist

Interior design by Nancy Deeks Buffington.

Le Marchand, the crown jewel of many Kopf homes and condominiums available for immediate occupancy.

As Cleveland's largest* residential home builder, Kopf Builders is the first choice of companies relocating professionals to Cleveland, Ohio. We currently offer 11 new home and condominium communities in Avon Lake and Westlake — the two most desirable communities in western Cleveland.

Kopf Builders, with over twenty-five years of building excellence, is your logical relocation choice. Telephone 216/871-8234 or 1-800-242-8913, Ext. 21.

THE HEAT & COOL PUMP Effective. Efficient. Economical. That's how people describe it.

Award Winning — Nationally Recognized
||||| KOPF BUILDERS

* *Professional Builder* magazine 1990 Top 400 ranking

Kopf Builders' Residence on the Beach offers waterfront views.

Devonshire Estates' "The Yorkshire"

extensive $37-million renovation.

City Plaza Hotel culminates an

The striking new lobby at Stouffer Tower

What's missing from these pict   es of Cleveland

UR missing out on the everyday enjoyment of a wide variety of distinctive floor plans and features like: wood-burning fireplace, in-suite washer/dryer, built-in microwave, fitness center with tanning bed, racquetball or tennis, pool, clubhouse and entertainment center — and all the other things that you would expect in a luxury apartment!

Our "Business Center" offers FAX, copier and other business support services for residents. Plus, you'll benefit from the care and commitment to service of our professional staff.

The Apartments at The Woodhawk Club

Sturbridge Square

inest apartment communities?

THE POLO·CLUB of Strongsville

14400 Howe Road
Strongsville, OH 44136
(216) 572-6555

THE APARTMENTS AT
THE WOODHAWK CLUB

180 Fox Hollow Drive
Mayfield Hts., OH 44124
(216) 646-9000

Three Cleveland-area locations.
Models open daily. Call for
directions and hours.

The Polo Club of Strongsville

Zaremba
managed communities

Relocating

with our free Relocation Service

We'll help make transferring easier

Getting transferred often means a big promotion, but it can also involve a lot of complicated problems. To make it easier on you and your family, we've collected information about local realtors, banks, furniture, short-term accommodations, and many other issues related to your move.

We understand what you're going through and know exactly how to help. Call toll free anywhere in the United States and ask for our Relocation Director

Katy Morgan. She'll be happy to send you the information you request, free of charge.

So call the number listed here. The information is free. The help...invaluable.

1 - 8 0 0 - 2 3 4 - 2 4 5 4

Serving Akron, Canton, Cleveland, Ohio
Erie and Pittsburgh Pennsylvania.

Monday-Friday 9 am-5pm

Provided for you by
City Visitor®
Publications